Under the Big Span of Small Regards

Jamey Jones

SPUYTEN DUYVIL

New York City

ACKNOWLEDGEMENTS

Thanks to the editors of the following journals for publishing some of these poems: *Fellswoop: The All-Bohemian Review, Backdoor Poets, brown box, The Mundane Egg*, and *Mesachabe: The Journal of Surregionalism*.

Special thanks to Richard Martin for getting the ball rolling, Joel Dailey for thinking this was a good idea and pestering me to see it through, Rachael Pongetti for her editorial prowess, and Tod Thilleman for making it real.

My gratitude, in memoriam, to Phyllis Cook for being my friend and allowing me to make books after hours, Charlie Warner for his guidance, kindness, and healing pace always, Bernadette Mayer for her introduction to *The Derby Earth*, and Amiri Baraka for showing me how to begin.

for my grandchildren:
Dylan, Dawson, Tryfan, Macsen, Gwynne, and Alys

CONTENTS

July: A Meditation On Ted Berrigan (1994)   5

the middle time (1997)   19

blockhead (2003)   47

The Derby Earth (2003)   57

the notebook troubled the sleep door (2003-2004)   87

If You See An Ocelot, Please Remove This Letter (2006-2007)   113

Telescope (2002-2010)   153

The seven chapbooks gathered here are early attempts at getting my poetry beyond the notebook and out into the world. This process began with *July: A Meditation on Ted Berrigan*, which came from notes I took while reading *So Going Around Cities* for the first time. I was new to his poetry and that collection joyfully blew my mind in ways difficult to describe. I was happy with the notes, and could see them as a chapbook, which is something I'd wanted to make ever since meeting Amiri Baraka two years earlier as a student in the Jack Kerouac Summer Writing Program at Naropa University in Boulder, Colorado. At that time, I had no idea who Baraka was, but within my first hour there I noticed a man in an over-sized blazer with a bag hanging over one shoulder on the campus lawn. He was selling little zine-like books to students, so I approached him and asked how much. "Two bucks," he said, and we made our exchange. The book was titled *Boptrees* and consisted of individual poems by him and his wife, Amina. It was simply produced: 8 ½ x 11, 20 lb. white paper folded in half, 2 staples in the fold. The cover was toner black and in that darkness was a number 5, an onyx, the title, and their names variously colored in with crayons. On the right side of the first poem, he wrote "For Jamey, it's our world 2. Amiri Baraka, 92', Naropa." I would soon learn of his legendary stature in the literary world, first by finding a shelf full of his titles in the campus bookstore soon after our meeting. Later that week I attended his reading, as well as a lecture in which he stressed the need for poets to make their own books instead of waiting for publishers to come knocking on the door. Two years later I followed his lead and made my Berrigan notes into a book: 8 ½ x 11, 20 lb. white paper folded in half, 2 staples in the fold. On the cover was the title, my name, and a crude drawing of Ted, each copy individually colored with crayons by my 6-year-old daughter, Maya. I made roughly 50 copies and carried them everywhere—readings, punk shows, the Y, the grocery store, etc., and sold them for—you guessed it—two bucks.

Over the next 16 years I made 6 more chapbooks and promoted them in the same manner. This was all a long time ago. It's quite strange, yet satisfying, to have them together in one book. They chart the path of a much younger me, for better or worse, living through the poems, experimenting, striving to be authentic, and taking my chances. I'm not that guy anymore, but I relate to him and appreciate what he was up to. Here's to the path. Onward!

July:

A Meditation on Ted Berrigan

(1994)

unnerved under stars
there's a few shortcuts
from Fred's house to
Strega Nona's

we slept
then woke
tired of poetry readings
and with a thirst for something new
we woke as we woke
not really bothered by anything
not excited, not unexcited
we woke
REM has a cool song called
"We Walk"
Ted Berrigan has a poem called
"A Boke"

fourth of July weekend
and everyone is hoping for
"good weather," as in hot
humid swamp beer hamburger
grilled fireworks sunshine
American flags sweat heat
red meat American
by birth   starter fluid
charcoal by the grace of god

but instead
here it is, July 3, Sunday morning
and Tropical Storm Alberto
is 160 miles south/southeast
from our Pensacola panhandle plan
60 mph winds, "tremendous storm surges"
expected, and possible tornadoes
the beach is being evacuated
and many people are pissed
that this "awful" and "nasty" weather
is threatening the Fourth of July
festivities, but I feel fine
and see the weather
as supreme
an atmospheric gift
in which to contemplate
the idea of tomorrow being
not only the anniversary of 218 years
of American independence
but also the day Ted Berrigan
died, eleven years ago.

A perfect way to pass the time
because it's Ted
who I read in my heart
and head
here on a couch
with coffee
3 AM or thereabouts
watching the weather channel
volume muted
hearing the wind
pick up
outside

have a glass of water
turn on the blue world
light a stick of incense

Tropical storm Alberto
was really a tropical
wimp
but the fresh winds
are nice
making my front yard
palm tree dance slow
and elegant
with its cubist wooden
horse at its base
the one Fred and I long ago
retrieved from a trash pile
on the roadside
originally thinking it was
a lawn mower
it's lower to the
ground
   then it used to be
it rots a little more year by
year
  day by day
an integral part of our
yard
yard art picture
it reminds me of a Picasso
painting out there
under the billowing palm
I wonder if Picasso ever
painted a palm tree
or a wooden horse

you must have cotton socks
and boots on your feet
when trying to write poetry
here in mosquito land
when it's 4th of July
fireworks and wind
not too distant
thunder rumble
rain clouds
clouding over, threatening
to wet the parade, marsh
the band wagon, wetland
the Pensacola Symphony
Orchestra and the 1812
Overture
here in swamp world
swamp time
in this land of our free
we're quite brave to be
at home
sitting
on the
front porch

because I write poems
like hair breathing out of
my skin at which point the
every little bit and tip
begins to glow and dance
like a ballet of memory
a tribal jaunt and rant
of genealogy, I swish
and swash in the puddles
of my lightness, at last
connecting

this is not meant to be
political philosophy
but I suppose it could be

actually it's "Chinese Nightingale"
actually its "Wrong Train"
actually "Around the Fire"
actually "In the 51st State"
actually "Things to do in Providence"
quite likely my favorite book
is *So Going Around Cities*
and I am here
so going around swamps
so living in my own time

July 7 Conversation Between Me and Fred

"you can't sell used cars to a baby goat"
"you can't find your refrigerator at
Montgomery Wards because the people
who work there can't find their own assholes"
"it takes an act of bravery to get out of bed"
"and compasses for shoestrings"
"and mouthfuls of magnolia leaves"
"ears talking streetlights'
"noses full of yield signs"
"yardsticks"
"slide rule"
"annotated history of crayons"
"fish squirrels"
"prozac assault spiders"
"prozac pizza parlors"
"comas parked on the roadside"
"coma toasted"
"coma toast and jam"
"crumpet wax"
"telephone erection squeeze"
"the dating game"
"let's make a deal"
"okay, shoot"
"Salvador Dali Lama"
"Bingo Pajama"
"Yorkshire Terrier cigarette lobotomy"
"foggy black ghosts chanting spiders"
"two in the morning doughnut self-absorption"
"sugar train"
"vegetable guitar"
"aluminum compost memory"

"corn stalk stupas"
"renaissance sunflower hair"
"manhole"
"womanhole"
"one of your headlights is out"
"one of your eyelids is skewed"
"if I don't see you in the future I'll
see you in the pasture"
"if I don't see you tomorrow I'll
 see you last year"

the middle time

(1997)

she slept on a mat on the
floor   unsure of the desert
within her

1

slightly up her dress
major cities end in dust
a cardinal in the fog
on the morning of

everything Christmas
and all those who believe
that the poet and the
fisherman are friends

go to bed alone, cold
and ill saying wouldn't it
be convenient if we could
just be in love   colder

however, she is agreeing
with me   in the middle time

2

by it all   Llisa keeping
it alive, family structures
falling down, yet Christmas
shambles have a beauty all

their own and Christmas is
invented   Bing Crosby
invented white sadness
every time I hear   the train

whistle blows just in the nick
of time   "what did you get
your husband for Christmas"
"a drum"   quite perfectly

sad silent work ethic blues
at the end of a thick year

3

Eratosthenes discovered
the circumference of the
earth   Fred's in Spain
discovering the circumference

of Spanish windows through
the lens of a pocket camera
I see beautiful women
fly right on by

right on   she wears lots
of eyeliner in the fog
and is miles away
in an unknown direction

she is flowers growing on
a cold foggy distant shore

4

I am a man of enormous
evolution and my world
crumbles and rebuilds itself
a million times over   living

flowers written all over your
your face   beautiful girls all
of a sudden turned sexy in the
middle of the mall   dropped

right out of my mouth   in the
grand scheme of things   every time
I don't take a shower I love Rene
even more   the comfortable grime

becomes us in the funk of our
daily hunkering down

5

earlier it hung low
now the wind blows
with rain what the sea
does yesterday   like

lingering long-dead
marriages   drops of water
hang   toasty is a good word
don't think I'm into name-

brands though skies will
open as her lips are a near
perfect red   so much more
than gravity is saying

I encounter storms whenever
I sit and breathe

6

learn to ride a unicycle
I'm in a cemetery
from another side
and divorced from Wynona

both died in 1919
a great year for sparrows
the earth is full of torture
and wonderment

oak trees and Johnny Depp
remind me of them
the cool graves of girls
who I don't even know

missing homesick at lunch
blue women in love with my skin

7

a distant thought like
subtle cathedrals keeps coming
around at dawn in my
mind's early music

no big deal but women I've
never seen haunt me and are
keen like strange cats in
the streets of Spain

where Fred measures the
circumference of windows in
the rain   a harrowing absence
within my being comes to surface

I need light and prayer
and painless songs from air

8

"read on," said last night's
harrowing splurt   horrible poets
should stay home in bed with
the lights out   don't be cruel

blue mirrors reflecting
Beethoven's thoughts like
the nets of sheer spirits
Indian hunters on the beach

which are not present
in the air I read on Sunday
evenings when dust collides
with my rebel emotions

god gravity pain the source
of all banks like hellish vacuums

9

things are at a bigger plan
than I am   hungry angels
running in circles in the wind
clown mammals of gravity

I imitate what I see until
it becomes me   and then
I wear it well   like the
smell of the gulf at dawn

I wanna' get lost and
shatter   something found
true one day while waking
up warm   nothing is enough

and everything begins, sings
and moans, just like the Ramones

10

sun also rises   blending
and calling in colloquial
tongue, "the goose has died"
as Lou Reed's sister for

a Pensacola minute struts through
the park, a tough fucking
artist in love with her details,
she makes art from air

she must find total liberation
even if only at lunch
downtown pelicans over sleepy
beer bottles of different shades

of blue say sweet "I love yous"
to her sublime presence

11

subliminal is not sublime
you know that by now
pulling my heart apart
with invisible signs

the sun so much I most often
bleed a spark   of mentality
glistening   of energy
93,000,000 miles away

of a Monday paid   but not
yet laid   in every poem
a big "fuck that"   so
blindingly   "may you

be forever strange   may
neither spring nor ashes faze

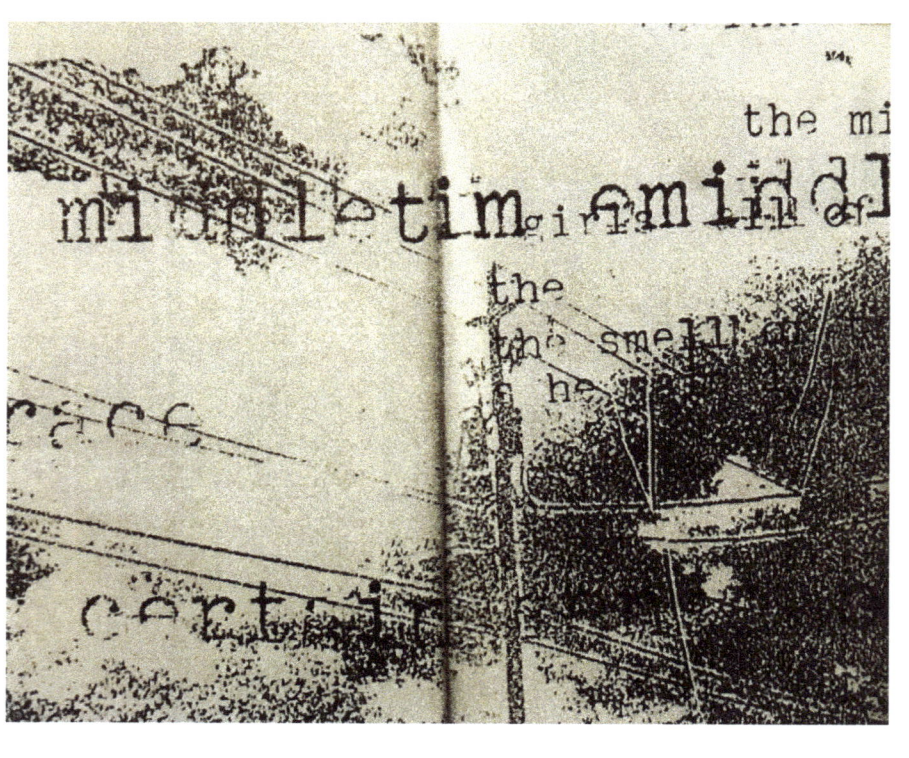

12

your dailiness"   dishwasher
sounds like a mechanical water
fall as David Byrne's windshield
wipers make perfect sense

paranoid, check the doors
or employing atomic energy
in dreams to have guns
in the nuclear sky

with his fellow cold-blooded
Spaniards   I am very attracted
to my escort as she leaves me
in the darkness, however, Steve

drives deep into work like an
eggplant missile heading west

13

under the pecan tree King
Louis looked it up and
every god fell from grace
slightly, only to rise

higher than before   west, he
headed deep into unemployable
habitat to lay down the seeds
of a vast new beauty

solid and bountiful, his poetry
became more obscure by the
milliseconds and the ever-changing
fields of his alone were

grandly transformed as he began
to see, truly, what time it was

14

taking in the sun
the helper gets the paint
and wrestles with his
genitals to pass the time

she said I didn't have
what it takes to make
a family work   what we
learned also is a jar of

dreams goes a long way
when you're weak and scared
stick to it   the mind behind
to symbolize the check

book   mundane and surreal
everything is symbols

15

hand forever what it is
kiss the goldfish on the
mouth, "shit, you melted
my butter this side of

the moon"   sitting on the
the dock of the bay
93,000,000 miles from the sun
it's the same with horses

as it is with bosses
and sleep comes like
heavenly rain slightly up
her dress the mind smiles

major cities end in dust, cardinal
in the fog, more than minor

16

in the middle time
she slept on a mat on
the floor   unsure of
the desert within her

a cardinal in a minor
city in the fog is more
than dust   heaven agrees
just kissing the goldfish

into melted butter   slightly
up her dress   horses
and bosses   93,000,000
miles are nowhere

to be found   cooked in
the sun we find water

17

cooked in the sun we
find water slightly up
her dress where everything
so mysteriously begins

the struggle of the new life
of a hangover can grow into
an awful plant by day's end,
though we whistle in our

sadness   even in the worst
of days madness passes
like in the morning when
the clatter won't rhyme

a small sense of grace   here
in the middle time

18

when the clatter won't
rhyme we inherit a
small sense of grace
from unmetered air

raw like music, the
unsayable is always said
and so rarely heard
as a hammer or a bird

word for word our lips
make shapes for passing
life sounds   strangers
come from nowhere

anywhere the same, the
evolution of communication

19

naked in the atomic
world the dancers were
denied entrance into the
grand watering hole

within as the ceiling breathed
the dance floor melted and
all became one in the form
of one   a revolutionary

in a clumsy war
the artists were stuck
at the door and nothing
is ever what it seems

it was a matter of seeing
it always is   anytime

20

any time of day it's good
to make work work
to take dust and make
light   major cities

rise, even on the most
minor days we are all
inhabitants of the wild
world and we live in our

dreams   faucets drip and
cats are eccentric   a separate
breed   walking planets
in fur   lots of style

like Bukowski said
now he's dead

21

the uncomfortable grime
becomes us in our daily habit
of hunkering down   we are sexy
blues reuniting in funeral

homes in the badlands
stranger than fiction
we become each other as
our worlds crumble

and rebuild themselves
over and over a million
times   you'll do any time
loving you is a cinch

even in a pinch turned sexy
in the middle of the mall

22

in here the middle time hangs
all over me like dolphins
in the air, sky blue, water
bluer   on postcards

like a tarp dirty with physical
songs and blue collar musings
doodles in the fog   a time to
remember   and a time to

just think   a time to build
families and a time   to sink
here time means little like
a French Quarter statue

that's really a mime, we hang
in the air   of the middle time

blockhead

(2003)

traveler

blockhead

Leonardo Bigollo

Tapped into nature

What's in the air, everywhere

Did he notice it first outside of himself?

Or from the inside did something stir,
begging to come out? Tiny heartbeat.

By observing the birth patterns of rabbits something clicked. A
light arrived. Patterns seen in many things. Sunflower. Pineapple.
Starfish. Daisies.

In northern Africa he learned the decimal system of numerals.
Clouds shifting in a massive sky. He was hungry for found things
and took delight in finding them. People thought he was nuts.
Whacko!

Whacko Fibonacci! Who dreamed prophetic Hindu Arabic!
He wrote a book encouraging the use of that numeration system
called, "Liber Abaci" (A book about the abacus). In it he
explained the birth patterns of rabbits. Scoffed at by his critics for
his interest in new numbers, for his new and strange rabbit
inspired numerical insights.

forwarded the patterns within the sunflower as a map as a code a spirograph design when I was a kid and had no idea of the mathematics of it but knew everything I needed to know I suppose just like Harry Smith saying, "Found art is everywhere" so the blockhead Leonardo had an epiphany and found a sequence in front of his nose a new language on his fingertip a dust fleck in his brow a numerical sutra somehow a new light already in place waiting to be found.

I

N

In

In a

Shift

Shifting

Pattern of into

And out of, motion and light

In a shifting pattern of into and out of, of

A shifting pattern of into and out of, of motion and
light, a shifting

In a shifting pattern of into and out of, motion and
light, a shifting, a new dream of numbers blowing
in the wind

L eonardo tapped into the numbers in most
E verything, this certainly must have been
O verwhelming and delightful.
N evertheless, his new numbers
A dded up, made sense, even though they were
R abbit-inspired, makes no
D ifference, these were the numbers
O f nature, just waiting to be found

F lowers and freaks are eccentric
I ncidents frequently happening everywhere
B ig ideas, the stranger the better, going
O ver everyone's head, genius is
N ever easy, though
A dding the previous two to get the next is
C oncise and simple, at once
C oncrete and flexible, like
I ncidentals in the day world

B igollo means 'traveler' and 'blockhead'
I 'm wondering how it could mean both
G reat things happen all the time but
O nly some of them get the attention they deserve
L ove is really having one's eyes open and
L eaning forward, pushing ahead, even when afraid
O r simply delighting in a thought or idea

B ound to the patterns of travel
L over of skies, the blockhead,
O f Italian blood, he was
C razy for numbers, his
K een observations were profound, inspiring
H im to go further
E ven though some thought he was a joke, they couldn't
A ppreciate what he was up to, not having the
D epth and imagination to keep up

I

N

In

In a

Remem

Remember

In a remembered

In a remembered dream a sh

In a remembered dream a shifting pattern

In a remembered dream a shifting pattern in reverse,
out of and into

In a remembered dream a shifting pattern in reverse,
out of and into, motion, light, numbers blowing
backwards

found art as a way of counting keeping score knowing the time of day forecasting the weather learning the flight patterns of birds and why leaves fall the way they do or take the birth rate of rabbits for instance the light of it says one one two then three five eight for infinity the gift of Fibonacci the discoveries of blockheads the commonality of the pineapple starfish sunflower or any composite flower such as the daisy or aster bird shadows passing flashes of shade in light in air

Backwards in a time stance the Japanese Magnolia petals fell up from the ground, eight five three two in as many days as it took the ground to dry, mocking bird subtracting each two previous beats to complete the next, the world of backyards is made up of numbers, any ole' blockhead can see that

Backwards to a past time show me numbers and I see numbers show me sunflowers and yes the scattered stars and their histories the patterns of birds in flight, sets, groups, relativity bending, reeling

His father was a customs manager in the mercantile business, which enabled young Leonardo to experience and explore the Mediterranean world

Born in Pisa, he was also called "Leonardo Pisano"
(or Leonardo of Pisa)

Before his birth, what were numbers to him?

The shifting light, inside, outside

Blurred numbers, waking

Leonardo Bigollo

blockhead

traveler

The Derby Earth

(2003)

Many thanks to the possibilities—Scotty-the-potty-boy Satterwhite and his world—the Sub-City tribe and everything they're about—Vic Chesnutt for his CD *left to his own devices,* which pretty much was the soundtrack for "The Derby Earth"— also, his rambling proem in the liner notes inspired the physical form, odd spacing, and overall nature of the poem—Bernadette Mayer for her tintinnabulating intro., lucky me, I feel like a chipmunk—Chris Davis, a door is a door is a short door—my sister, Llisa, for her eyes and the way they see—and of course, Rene and Ansley, who are a little older now and, now that the text is complete, are leaving Derby (finally), and advancing to Lawrence (part II), in further search of psychology and the ghost of William Burroughs—good luck kids.

Cheers, J. J.

for Rene

Introduction

the transparent trees of derby, kansas   midnight

   bicycle game sequence   the food swamp teepees

secret houston   i heard the position of our heads flirting

with rene and theosophy   it was a trick my friends proved

  pensacola quietude   upside down chipmunk at the birdfeeder

and and and perpetual faster & faster to the scene of the

disaster   like dreams steer cops and tricks   ansley too

  a pavilion suggestion whacks the form   then a terminal heart

lions a charged leopard   oozing quietude like days of bells

even rene   walking for the first time once   oak trees

  incessant oak trees pervading our dreams like tintinnabulating

goldfinches   here here   i they i me though we amortize

   polar scholars are supine now   come in & dream of derby

with me   don't miss the departing pizza   nothing pizza

proxy proximity pizza   herewith pizza with fresh figs

we'll be observing forewith   lost magic hat   pink gulf

  his pinkish oranges   and and and astutely driven smoothness

wait!   wizards cry guilty plus walmart   we almost tread there

   bicycle game sequence   patchouli smells like missing

all the wheat of an eden or internet   eyebrow gigantic eyebrow

  time weight   time me

---Bernadette Mayer

day

DERBY DAZE

4 days till Derby
Derby in a nest bag
67037 a Derby zip nod
A Derby eye blink
What's the code of Derby
The code underneath the code
The Derby underneath the Derby
The song within the song
Derby could be dream-like
How many Debbies live in Derby
One Ansley and one Rene
Landed in Derby way before yesterday
And will remain so for a
Good while after tomorrow
Tomorrow done did to Derby
What the Duke did to dinosaurs
Derby diphthongs divided by dimes
Equals Ansley's a Derby diplomat
Derbiful
Derbiage
Derbier
Derbies
Derby soup
A Derby hat
The Kentucky Derby
The Soap-Box Derby
Let's all go on a Derby hunt
Kansas love triangles drawn in the dirt
Call your friend and have a Derby flirt

Derby gossip coming through the wires
Play phone-tag with Derby
Derby does a striptease and gets
Sent home from school
Hello, wake up, we are the cult of Derby
The flatlands of Derby
The flatbed trucks of Derby
Derby El Caminos in the rain
Derby trains wisely smile on
All the transient human types
Dancing to the music of Derby
The soundtrack of Derby
Gimme' some Derby skin, man
Derby hardware can you hold please
Derby undercover
Derby in the air
Between the bed sheets of Derby
The Derby world of sex
The sex life of Derbians
"How I Became a Derbian and
Other Creation Stories,"
By one Ansley Patrick
Eating cereal in Derby
Feeling super surreal in Derby
Derby in a nutshell
Derby on a fingernail
Derby like Whoville
Tracing the history of the mud puddles of Derby
Love and war in the Derby streets
Vote Ansely Patrick to be your friendly Derby Mayor

Ansley, born to be a Derbian
Rene, born to be Rene
Doing time in Derby
I will sing throughout the fields of Derby
I will haunt your Derby streets and make
Sure your Derby hair does not get ruffled
In the Derby wind and rain
Derby like one big golf course
Derby flat and windy
Derby hidden
Derby lost
Derby slightly sexy and a little horny
Furtive Derby when did you forget you were furtive
Derby then, Derby now
Derby about to be

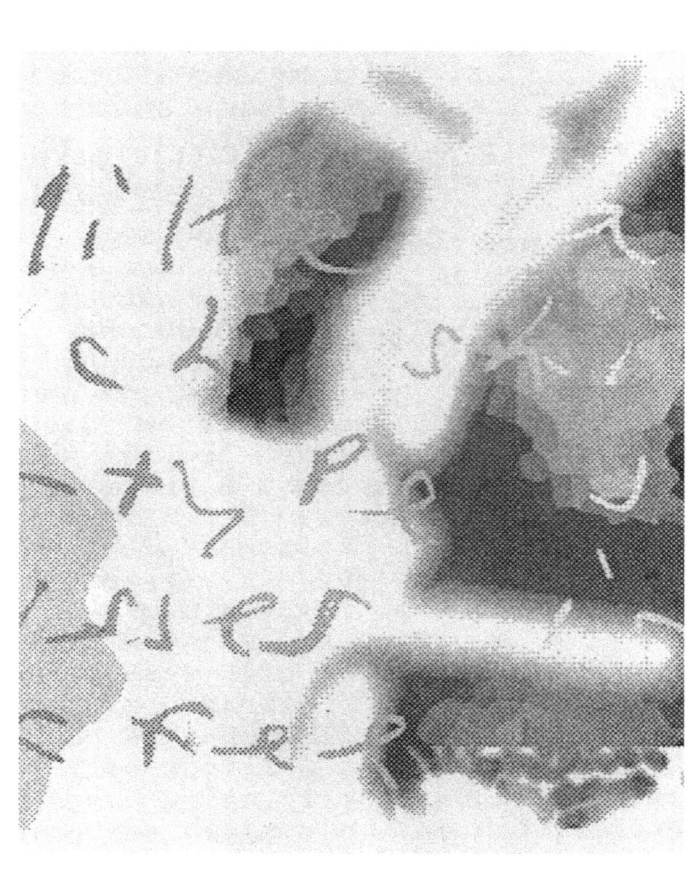

8/21/2001

I walk up on a scene, several people surrounding
William Burroughs lying face-up in an open
coffin. He's alive and awake, eyes open. As
I approach someone says to him, "Jamey's
here," and they all part to let me through.
As usual, he's in a suit and tie, fedora on his
chest. He looks up at me with one of the most
tender smiles I've ever seen. I say, "Hello Bill,"
and bend down to lightly kiss him on his left
cheek, after which he continues to smile.
His eyes glisten, and his cheeks are rosy.
He's happy to see me.

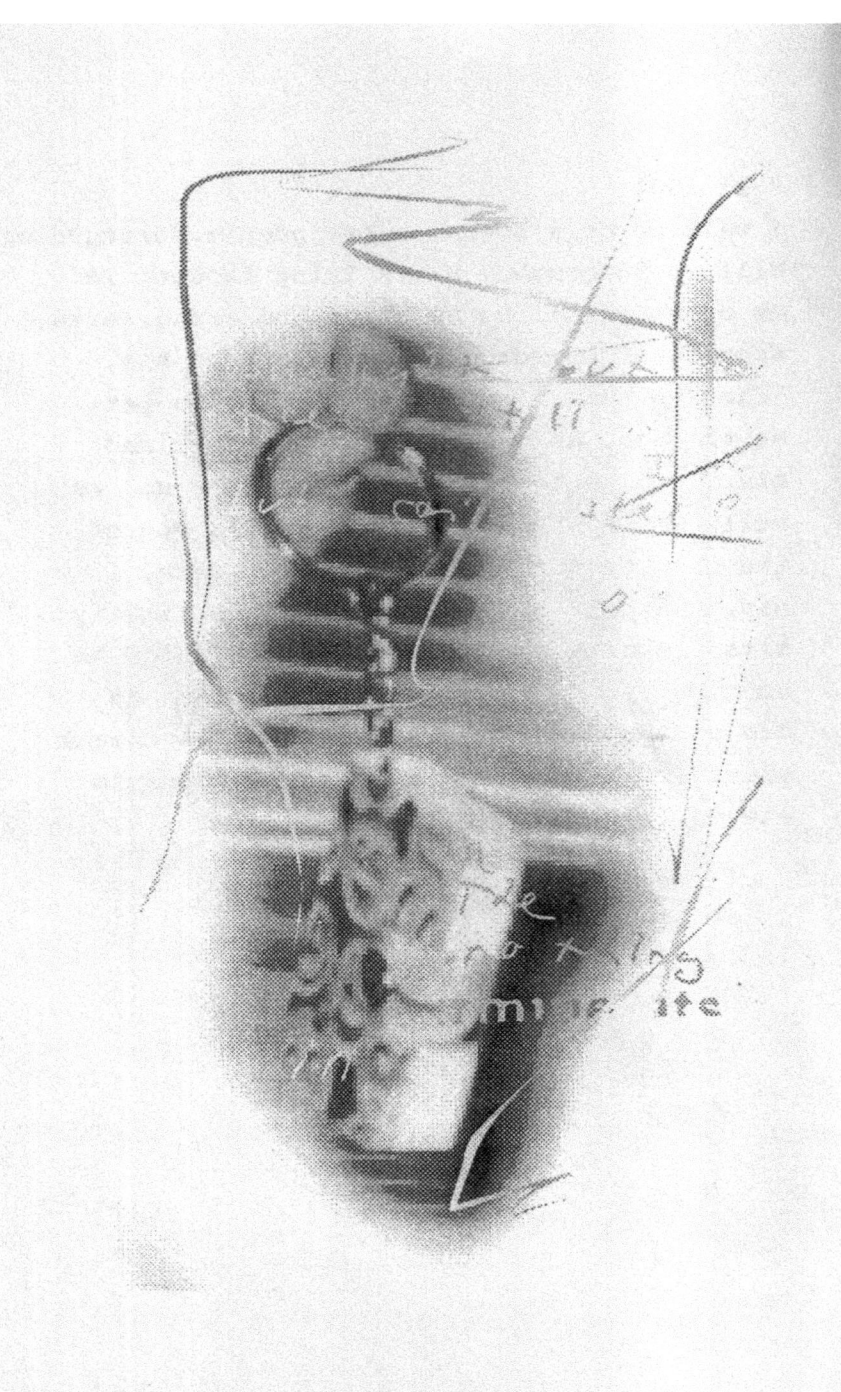

The Derby Earth

"Language, language
black Earth-circle in the rear window"
Allen Ginsberg, "Wichita Vortex Sutra"

back from kansas dry   wichita   derby   texas   houston   kansas
dry hot cracked flat and weighted down   rene seemed bugged and
bothered by me or something i did or was doing or will do she seemed
in a stew   perhaps it was because i only came for 48 hours instead
of 72   i said i think i'll take a bath and she looked at me like that was
a weird thing to say   looked at me like she wasn't saying what she
really wanted to say   what was in her heart to say   i could have
flown out her front door right then and up above the cracked yard
and   into   the derby american evening breath of sky   that is if i
could fly   what   in   of   sideways word-thought   question come
kum-n-go   bang and blame   squirt and flirt   walking later in the
hothouse derby nature trail ansley declared "it's not fair" that there is
more than one path to choose from   rene said that not everything in
life is fair   the game of life exuded walloping colors   ansley revealed
his inner-insurance salesmanship   i begged a tired born again bone
yard jetlaggedeness as i lagged behind learning the ropes of cash-
cropped property cards   popping stouts one after another one   1
2   3   awaken in wheat field anomalies and the skies are edified with
free-floating overweight air force planes and monogamous hawks   in
the forcefield strains of american dust ghosts   floating backwards
the ships hit home with little or no resistance   as stouted in dreams
and prisons of things buckled to and fro   i heard the train asleep that
night   in g g's room   a little bugled and clown-like was the sound
compared to home and later the next day and day after that i noticed
they still have those colorful glass bells on the telephone poles along
the tracks   village inn oh village inn we pillaged in at lunch for
breakfast then and people-watched to witness the weighted wonder of
gloomy loops on all the faces   as if nothing could fully happen here

or was it my eyes   partial smiles and partial no-smiles   as if the
air the weight the blip of stateward squeeze   keeps us and them
and all the other fellows and felicias partially living like an existence
of everything partial and no slack remaining the glue comes true in
my morning runny nose and tired smile under crabapple car load-
ings   load em in   load em out   ansley has a most magnificent
dusty derby rock collection in a shoebox in the back seat of which
he has astutely learned and studied and felt the bodies and tips and
seemingly memorized the shapes and the textures   and he quizzed
me constantly on things such as these as we drove the hay-field miles
and rene said "he got em' in the driveway"   an eye for light in the
shadows of giants   under the noses of ancient little five year old
men   eye blinks   all for feeling   of   rock   from a crabapple
driveway path   pieces of history   the archaeology of arcaneness
he is a wizard an elf   a point   in a pointless universe   hope like
oranges   in kansas an orange is an alien thing   but an orange like
hope   thinking i was doing good i made the coffee but rene cried
crime   once she stepped slurped pulled suctioned away from her
mouse and modem   and was like damn you put four scoops instead
of three grrr   leaving me loose and kansas guilty   for overstepping
the coffee boundary   reprimanded rubber banded confounded and
zoological   ansley said his mom was a psychology   i think i would
have to agree   mornings in derby were dreamy   the david lynch
safety zone   free like dharma bum cool breezes   and post-world
war two smilings a lightness of where america could come from   a
weary of a would-be   the tight ships of nebraska   the flatlands of
theosophy   timely soup yet prior to the what apocalypse   would
come to be   now is then   but once again   wooded centuries
turntable trouble   i would like to walk the derby streets in morning
cold   but cool became heat   and heat became song became blount
a wa wa wa walk in the park   those are my neighbors they live here
no more   they were mean that's all their stuff   out by the road

they let trees glide into the house   the people of derby cried crime
and finger-pointed ick immoral   at the park me and my fearless
loving leader   a diplomat at five in the strength of his mother's
watchful face   ansley wansley of impish universalness   played on a
crane   or some haiku version of one   imitated sand scooping he is
ansley of the dittish derby park by god the god-like and the warring   i
walked on a slanted chrome angle holding on to the coping   it was
luminous geometry   letting go and sliding down   how could you go
in a place so round   a village so stewy and held in   down to the
ditch fascinated by the no-water it holds   crossing like hot troops we
made our way to the two-toned merry-go-round and ansley almost
stepped on some hot gooey orange melted candy thing so moved to a
different place on the metal   a sound ship   a face heat   the rising
of the freakish freedom fields   i stepped stouted one two   it was a
lug experience   like pushing a dead leftover army tank in the bad
memory of model war glue   the orange stuff oozed as i heeded in the
hot sand round and round and rounded rounder in the sky middle
ansley held on and said faster faster faster faster   i dreamed again
perpetual roundest in the scheme we remain laboriously below slow
motion   weighted with army tanks   the hollows amongst us were
filled with lead blue in the brown grasses   ansley eyes the boy-chief
peddling past the water fountain before assuming his position on the
swing   bone for bone   the two hawks above our heads had exceed-
ed remote control   nothing fixed and all things extra   i pushed
ansley in wondrous whoa   felt of upward gravity   pull back load
down   fall upward   assuming   austerity   swinging like two
whips we never reached the trees due to the raining heat   derby
dharma defined   a social please me license plate club   family van
glue clots as i stopped took stooped blew myself into a foamed nap   i
dreamed the dream of the famed social irritator the forward psyche
manipulator   dreamed he was back   in the house   that derby built
nothing noted   undone   a new nouned lesser time   like verbs the

dream-light always dimmer   derby time   and sat himself at the
computer rudely and arrogant his fingers trespassed the keys to rene's
established eyebrows   derby lack-light   a fading   in an instant fade
new ship in an old field   dream loot   the cattle   the hay rolls
the freely free of the buffalo hills   hoofed to new details   time sent
we hovered   in speed limit   rene drew a line   the laws of walmart
walled in   together   the day began   an afternoon glow too hot for
hope   ansley said can i stay in the car   his mom said nope   the
dope of do-good chrome shopping carts   a cradle of cool-to-the-touch
basking in grocery we drooled to the one hour photo blank   i blinked
to fuji   a tired floor the hundreds walk on   groggy groans and
watered senses sedated someone vomited all over aisle nine we almost
tread there   ansley wanted to see   rene steered the buggy clear and
headed for the cola silences   steer me steer me cried the boy   the
old man boy the boy old man   olden begun before cop sense collided
my dad's a police cop is my dad dead   people see science in afternoon
sad light middle america   i held hard to the wheel the back of his
neck   fitted my hand   a vehicle in a modern pretend creek   we
retailed away of our own devices   weaving in and out of the billowed
families and the partial foot falls we call home   near missing the big
butts   don't put my head in a butt you almost put my head in a butt
the strawberries   where's the throw oh no this is fun   a ramble in
the vines for purses   the N on the door traded history for   new skin
in the crabapple trade   i napped a dream   a molded nuance
awakened   our guests are here   a nearness   a wiccan flow her
modern science   exuded smooth and clear on the fiction couch
desire for the new models of rocky horror image grain   all the wheat
of a midnight place   crunch teeth   a pale skin   eyeglasses fixes
bicycle gleams   a 26 year-old parts number   an ADD deep dirty
game we snapped pictures in an age of living room   truth sequence
the family flew in   arriving pizza   a peppered beef   and the quiver
of annotated football ready   patchouli and stout for the historic easter

girl   new light new proximity new proxy weather the birthday cake
sat perfectly on thaw   i remember it then   tip the candles off   they
antiquated the breezes and wonder of the streets of ancient tel aviv   i
hummed the note   bounded flaps the party became itself and sat in
big chairs   nibbling on wings and guacamole   what once came early
is now and once again   the once and future clicks of the addled neon
kum-n-go   what do the people think   what must the porno know
a knowing in a place state   the people punctuated the donuts here are
big   amongst the are river   of the are kansas the river itself a slow
bone secret   the nearness of the creek tonight   or the heated equa-
tions of the nature trailisms   talismans of the heat of a continent
conquered   a nation notified on hold   suits of heat and black-shirt-
ed august grind on   the people the people here are the people we the
people here are some people cried ansley   in his hot-forehead-where-
are-we-going-day   their music floated like dreamy mennonite hay
leering leery the eyes glanced seemed pained before their plates   per-
haps pained but by no means no more than partial under the weight
the open pavilion   a hello in shiny eyes   they resembled the car-
toons of watchtowers   the lambs the lions   the juicy fruit king   an
N on the door   the nature of derby   in america   a before   in a
well-suited war no more   the nodding eyes nod out   a place to keep
the heart's secret heart for scooby-dooed the millions scooted by like
gravy   i saw the sights i hearkened the tourist miles   the whacked
and the wigged-out via the internet   the monitor showed the
free-standing mushroom stones   the mountain mini-rock formed in
the middle flats   what's it doing here   she told me this used to be an
ocean   then floated up the garden of eden   they shall hide their
nudity in a masonic solidity   he hereby foretold   for the comings
of old   for his body to mingle to reside in a glass coffin in a chain
place   baywatch hawaii replaced the gigantic ball of twine   i swear
to my soul and a roosevelt dime   it would matter   if i could clatter
or perfect the notions of tv suggestion   i said let's watch saturday

night live and i got the nose point eyebrow bath water reprimand
triangulated jaw bone glare   the drowse-o-clock after 10 pm it's our
tv how dare you dare look in slo-mo' stealth bomber time   a b-52 eye
twitch sentimental wearing remote control trousers   an ouch zone in
a moving picture patch   forgive me for i am confused   like the back-
lash whip scream of the coffee imbalancing incident   incidental in a
forward weird   notions of nations calling time in an ancient ocean
bed   a place where gravity closes in and cuddles close   a sink to a
nestle level   a dust   strength in slow the airplanes gloat over the
all-you-can-eat fields   i homily you   coffee crime   what   is it
exactly that the air's churned up   who are we timely   martin luther
king is a road of ditch   a pitch forth wiser place   i dream it's mon-
day and the night before his death i dream i tell this dream to a young
jesse jackson   who won't have it   it's all in east hill   this ghostly
place of memphis this over-fingered kansas hole   the heavy silence of
the dirt cakes   cackled by lonely the living room whispered in
small-time tornados   ansley charged in crawl   an all-fours buffalo
forward romp   a winded little head of an old man cave   into me by
the tv   by the leopard chain   any ole where he'd wedge   his cup
into my bone-legged trapping device   insisting like houdini that he
be allowed to escape by his own little devices   let me try to get out
glitter straps   carved shoulders   you massage my feet   and you
message my head   a squishy little raisin face   the ear pool lessen
learning the head the couch flew early   the highways pointed endless
the 100 million glinted miles   the airport hummed   a random
search in the heart arcade of a parcel a package of flown seat steering
the frankenstein elf   straight to the melting water works   another
threatening of a big butt place   music   the tube   we crawled into
(a tube)   we're getting tubed   this is tubular   the gringo the
fellaheen   the roving equipage people   unbound from baggage
claim   i saw your face and symmetry   in the force-field of the
terminal   the blowing particled   clumsy   unified   of a lost float-

ing holding the weight   circumstance the bones of a nation   under
god   invisible   what once was an ocean heretofore we are   shall
then be an earth place   ghost wave languages in the haywire seeds
bones   matriculated wheat strains   particles perfect blew   bound-
ed   bit   bibbled   equipature   i hollow home   via houston
what happened here   a terminal lonely bolt with bags   wichita said
airport sad by belt by birth by hard-pressed   cloudy loot   bagged
in the mall-like stem-cell   dreamed heat and houston expectations
the strange flower ended up in your birth boop   by far a town   a
held in face   a code away   a leap   a leak   a leaf   a derby land
a sacred cushion   dried guac on the floor   her birth place   a base
romance   the window tower water word seeing it for the first time   i
logged in a figurative back patting   oodling my id until i found the
lead   leather corn fields and all   a flounder in a plastic suit   a
gift from a saint   a kansas grist of sainthood   wipingly toe-tied in
the tongued afternoon new stew the airport threw me into a random
search   nearing i love you nearing so long   a sandwich of good-
bye land   place face   friend time in search air   hope in hopeless
feeling   next time bushmills   i tubed sadly away and wiped out
tired a reeling humid soup   my hair hackled in kansas lung fill   i
drove my feet into the tube   sadly 30,000 feet up and houston never
sounded so bright   the place of bushy airports   all the bushes in the
place   a regular handshake beaver trick   this is trickular   tricky
vintage   a sad trick   my friends like old neighbors so glad to see
me   we drive off in a white beamer leaving the beavers back in the
bardo   houston oh houston you felt like a swamp   i welcomed
your wet   we speeded the swampy covered outskirts of the air-
port   in search of food   the kansas lockdown left behind   hous-
ton is an open sky swamp a mexican place of muted anomalies   we
swing through the trees   texas   indians transformed into tex-mex
mouth-water   teepees to tvs   bedrolls   in a future way gone   on
the way back we lowered the roof   and exceeded the elevation of

speed limit to the point it was no longer visible   cell phone said the
bushes changed the terminal gate   i thought of you back there with
all that wheat   as we sped through a good feeling houston   a grainy
home movie the way the night goes strange   a beer in the welcomed
texas scene   a blow float in the shape of a white convertible bmw   a
good life skull grace   this is called smiling in houston the sky agrees
belly full thank the monster dieties   i'm back in a swamp again   i
think of you and all that hay and corn   the dennis hopper blue velvet
derby streets   held   contained   deep breath   sigh out   kansas
and the sleep of its slow breathe in   houston   awake in a sky near
the gulf   in an order of release   just north of another south of the
border   and the way south music of   the corn-killed middledom
america zone   poof   the moan continues   are you mr. jones   the
whole plane's fluctuating for you with blankets in there it's time to go
home   kiss your houston on the cheek   she's a waver and a creamer
i dreamed of her once   cash in the crop the swamp warmed you well
a womanly wet in a mouth tent   come home   come and go   be
new goo in the plastered sense   a nuance in a blasted theater   look
down upon the big dipper   cuddle her stars   a scholar of polar glint
the lucky stars   air   an elbow below   smile   a map of lights
that deep dark down there should be a louisiana   all those town
criers unable to decode the maps and the cave-like clutter of their
languages   in the sky   the jazz miles seem to multiply   propagate
and fume   whirlwind where you been   basked backwards bountiful
forwards   the clock dropped in the soup   all supine and alone the
flight whiskey watered   people with gum and ridiculous bags of nuts
hanging off their belts   the attendants wearing imaginary night-
gowns   sexy in their pinkness   versus the population of pensacola
just arrived   dirt quietude   what chamber did we do   down in
the mind   a done dial   a wheat blather   the hangover of middle
america in the long lost fight for the gleam seeds   for love longed in
the lighted hinges of the shifting currents   the mutual gimps of gab

gawdernits of psychological common dirt   dirted dirt-fed derby dirt
in a magic hat trip   the whirling dervishes of the derby seeds   we
dance this way   way past the scenery   a new remain   solitude of
slack   days whack into more days   like one big musical collision
the solitude of thuds   and where the head in light devours the shoes
of its birthright   there i'll be   there you'll be   a weekend away on
earth   down in the mouth of a friend trip   48 hours of kansas seed
packed in lore   union   gone time   the flights of a nerve-wracked
the clues of a past life the day before departure   bam   rattle frames
of a strange flower union   who we become   only dirt pieces of music
sense   a sense of starlight   a sense of time   two days of whacked
tension   a commonality miff rift but hopefully no dead tunes no true
crimes   your skewed operas disperse in my head   there's a car in your
closet   its secret humble headlights still mingle with mine at all times

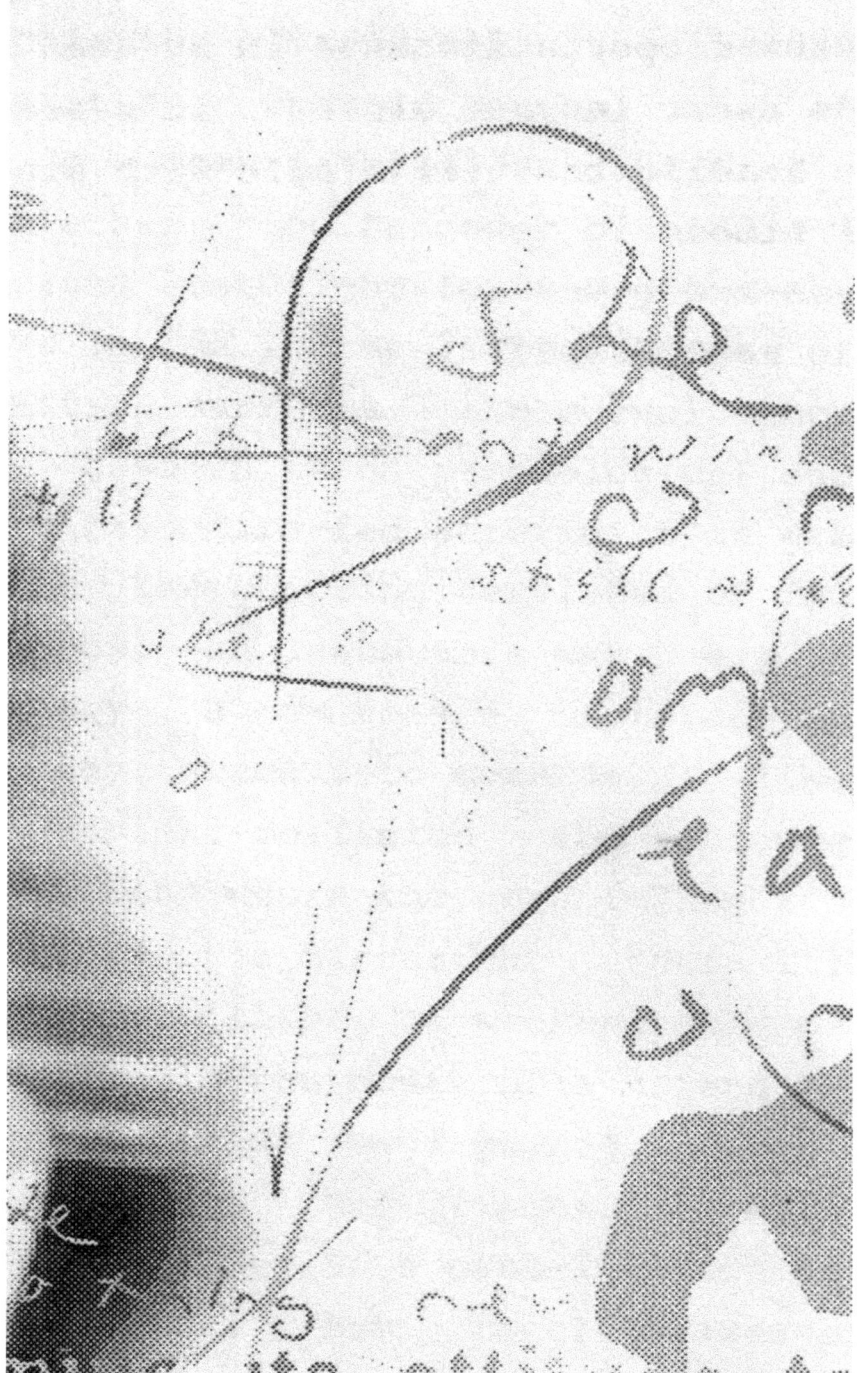

9/22/2001

Jack Nicholson and I are in Derby, Kansas. He's driving. We're going to Lyle's house. Apparently Lyle got my poem about Derby published, or at least had something to do with it. Soon after its publication it was banned in Derby. We drive to Lyle's so I can inquire. I'm on his porch knocking on the door. Jack's waiting for me in the car. It's a dark sedan like the one in Prizzi's Honor. After I knock once or twice I turn around to face Jack and the street. It's then I realize/remember that Rene and Ansley live directly across the street from Lyle on Derby Drive. I can see them through a lit window. We wave to each other. They come out. I leave Lyle's porch and walk toward them. We meet around Jack waiting in the Prizzi's Honor sedan. We chat. I introduce them to Jack. It's no big deal really. They tell me that Lyle's not home but the poem did indeed get banned. I get sort of excited. Jack does too. He takes the words right out of my head by saying, "Publicly, you could make this work for you." We drive off in Prizzi's Honor. I tell him I wrote "The Derby Earth" with Allen Ginsberg's "Wichita Vortex Sutra" strongly in my mind. He laughs in an approving way. I explain my impressions of Kansas and Wichita, but mainly of Derby, during the time I was writing it. He jokes sarcastically, saying something like, "O yea, like that predictable skyline over there." As I began to relate these impressions to him in greater detail, they seem to start proving themselves to be false. Everything I say I felt, saw, and experienced when I originally wrote it doesn't add up at all with what I'm feeling, seeing, and experiencing as we're driving along. I stick my bare toes in the dirt. It's wet, not dry. And unlike the Derby terrain but much like that of the south, there are lots of big oak trees, maybe some of the biggest I've ever seen. Behind some of the trees we see a big river, wide and deep. This is not the Derby I saw the first time. The oaks are all around. They're even growing sort of in the river, more to the side opposite of us. I begin to notice that some of these oaks are transparent. Inside of them, especially one that's very large, I can see the inner shell of the oak. The oak is hollow, as is the shell inside, rounded, like a domed cathedral space. Not so much a dome, but more like an orb. The inner orb of the Derby oaks. I never noticed them the first time around.

A DOG ABOUT ANSLEY

A dog about Ansley barking in
Kansas. It is no mystery as to
why the telephone is fading out
it is simply Rene walking out
to the fence of their backyard
to tell him to give that boy
his ball back the air is purely
Kansas.

As Ansley is greater than the traffic
of opinionated young teachers he's
more a call to the world of people
living existing and breathing as
the ways and the bays, bayous and
inlets within the fields of teacher
development.

He chased the boy with a stick
after he stole his ball then
threw the stick and hit that
girl on the map of her head.

That boy had originally agreed
to help Ansley over that big
fence to get to the basketball
court then Steve calls and says
I should go out to the Dock with
him to see Marcia Ball perform.
I say no and no again but like
mental backsliding ask

what time she starts
about nine he says
I say no again.

On the phone with Steve I told
him that Rene was American pissed
because she only had one stout
and that was in no way enough
to be British pissed.

Rene said Ansley was acting like
a jackass and Ansley in his old-man-
turning-toddler voice said, "I not
a jackass" and somehow this
recollection brings to mind old
washing machines.

"He's had a shitty week he's got
an abscessed tooth," she said and
the more I think of it now it was
the turning night air of Kansas
and the magic of fence borders
which probably only mostly seem
so to me at the other end down
here on the Gulf of where I draw
the line even though I've never
heard of her but trying to
imagine what she sounds like
I have no desire in the least
to go see Marcia Ball.

The basket's in place the chili
is simmering isn't Phil Jackson
from Kansas? She had a prowler
and 40 million other things happen
this week and now she has
heat-seeking missiles for floodlights.

They shot off for ten minutes the
other night so she called the cops,
cops of Kansas called in the night,
to find nothing but only to tell
her of the mentally challenged
thirty-something year-old man who
is a well-established peeping-tom
in these parts and that he knows
who all the single women are and
where they live.

I hurdle to think sometimes and
then there are movies about maps,
distance, time gaps, worm holes,
motion, landscapes and love. Thank
god the lonely too build TVs only
to turn them off.

After being busted in Kansas twice
by his mom for being mean and
stealing basketballs and throwing
sticks at limp and frail boys who
are bigger than him, Ansley's now
inside pleading, "I ready to be
good now," but then again this is

Kansas and she ain't the police
except when it comes to psychology
so yes she might talk about it
so like a termite he whittles
willing to find in the wildness
of the Kansas weight which
wood works.

A dog barking continuously in
Kansas during fade-outs and fade-ins
finding life fruitful in fence weather
she finds the well-established peeping-
tom online, "all sex offenders have
to be there you know."

But words float away so easy and
free that there are lapses of
straight-line silences from Kansas
to East Hill where fences for seconds
tiny dissolve and birds cock their
heads to one side her dead are all
around her at all times and her dad
left a rifle though she prefers
for defense, protection and overall
shamanistic and cosmological purposes,
a walking stick Fred created for her
years ago.

Light as in morning and years as
further studies in the sense of
stoically staying calm and alert,
it is possible for one to be in

a one-room apartment in Florida
and a backyard in Kansas at the
same time.

She will go out and buy wine now
then come home and raise her son.
The world will turn slightly or
greatly within earthly seconds
because in the issue of air and
from its perspective there is no
difference.

Kansas purely is air as the
necessity of time constructs
itself becomes revealed falls
flat like coke left open over
night.

The back ball of his boy that
give him seem suddenly like
new eyes to tell to him and them
of the magic force of fences and
their sleepy infiniteness.

The two out walking are really
one Rene and one ageless dude
she picked up along the way,
as Ansley, as a way of simple
unification. fission by numbers
and out-fading the telephone
the why to and how for it
dot com or the no mystery of

the shitty weeks and teeth
turned abscessed.

Brown fields and white sand
together meshed he chased the
boy frail and limp and taller
than he with a stick after
stealing his basketball planet.
The eyes tell stories and the
stars turn wet. Languages as
mapping systems, bent and
erratic trails lingering in
the wires as the day turns
night and a dog about Ansley
barks purely in Kansas.

the notebook troubled
the sleep door

(2003-2004)

Bernadette Before The Fog

Dreamed Harry Smith had a new book out.
On the cover were two copies of the same
picture of him staring straight at us, big
eyeglasses swallowing a rather shrunken
face.

It's true, I have a tendency toward religion.
Not so much the church but the dictionary
and the weeds in my garden. Palm fronds
flapping on the privacy fence make sense
to me in a way worth mentioning.

Bird mutterings, the absence of clouds, it
seems it's spring, it's an end of February
beginning. Plane rumble etches the edges
of who we are so we think to say something.
Or nothing. Sitting on a free couch in the pouring
sun almost makes me want to purr. The couch
is rotting and so are we, but first this news.

Coffee, green plastic patio decorum, fell swoop
eye charts bathe in the light, strands of spider web
like milk glisten pink then white, rising and falling
without losing composure. This at the height of
the privacy fence. A poet sits before the fog.
Is she smoking? Perhaps. Staring into the white,
does the free couch down the road take on new
meaning? Does it become a table? Or a sack
of mistakenly bad potatoes? A speedy sports car
new like a toothpaste commercial? Looking into the

fog, the couch could become a birdhouse I suppose, or a box kite, or damn near anything else, so long as it's free.

Stepping stones of perfect squares imperfectly placed between two palms on the shore. The line leads to the sound. The sound turns white. A poet sits in a plastic chair. Is Hector there? I'm sure he is, but I've yet to see him. One chair empty like an offering not an absence. Here space seems terrific as visibility stops at the end of the docks.
I see nothing. I see everything. How about you? The possibilities abound. The docks are perfectly straight but not foreboding.
Pine cones brown litter the earth like salt like fog like a mutual agreement minus snow. Pine straw reddens it all just enough to blink green. Someone said the fog is a sign of spring. It seemed strange at the time, but now I can almost see it.

A white order. A blue fog. How near are the blue herons to where she sits? And do they, like the free couch down the road, change forms in the new, yet ever-glorious, nothing morning? You bet! But no matter, here the couch is free of Bay Street, here the sound is just a thought. Blue-sky sun roasting my skin. An ending to February begins. An envelope jumps off the table. A fly thinks on my leg. A neighborly cat shifts through the drying grass. Time passes, leaving traces of itself

everywhere. Little things like the wine cork
in the bird feeder. Or the ashes from last
year, to show that friends were here.

But it all seems to work out. The old dreams
suddenly seem inseparable from the new ones.
The free range of the fog inhibits nothing.
The free couch hovers in its place. Where a
poet sits in a plastic chair, probably smoking.
Hector goes invisible, but he's funny like that.
The sun blasts everything to smithereens, a more
than welcome disaster that invariably lightens
the load. People walk around differently, in a
kind of cheerful daze, like waking up on a day
off. There's something funny about it. The new
light seems almost clumsy, as if testing itself.
The spaces fill in, making use of what's there.
It's great how that works. It's been a long time
coming.

ROARING CAMP

for John Ashbery

Umberto Eco left the boat show in a hurry.
You should have seen it. He blended in with
the general riff-raff as they exited the building,
but that's beside the point.

What I'm left with now is the memory of
how great the fire was the other night,
and more specifically how my page got
partially burned, stepped on, then much
later something was spilled on it, which actually
made it look like an ancient letter never sent.
After the night got through with it, it seemed
more authentic in a way, the Latin sentences
half burned, crumbling brown edges.

Thinking to accumulate images taken, culled,
received from the last few days of living, and
wanting to call it a threnody. I guess anything
could be that, if viewed with the right amount
of gray, I mean grace. But you know, I'm not
a butterfly, nor do I specifically care to be, so
when she started in on her pitiful sermon I had
to move, and without making eye contact with
anyone, I sauntered off in search of firewood.
Little did I know that your neurotic dog would
follow my heels and bark constantly like a maniac,
which I'm sure interrupted the thin air of her
words back at the camp. This gave me a laugh
though, and I just carried on, as if there was no

barking dog. I said to myself, "it is a good day
to ignore the barking dog."

The computer hums. It's a nightmare and a relief.
It holds the face of one Francis Thompson, whose
place in this world was vacated long ago, replaced
by his legacy—scads of poems and biographical data,
images and remembrances, lingering, preserved.
You would probably dig his poems.

The messages are indeed received penultimately.
It's about reception really. Like the way a pile
of rubbish all of a sudden will make sense,
or how you finally understand something you
said years ago, and wonder how in the hell
you even said it when you didn't know
what it meant. Big deal. It's always there
but not always noticed. A letter waits to be
written and sent. It's about a man with gentle
hands who died. It's not a sad letter, even
though it seems like one as I tell you about it.

I recall the haunted acreage at the foot
of the bridge. the toponymic sillies
of trash day in Beulah. The way we
met. It all adds up. It does connect,
but perhaps not today.

Like a dream of drinking beer made
from untreated wood. Or the way all
the houses behind us burned, but their
remains were not the remains of what

they had been, but something much
older and obscure, from another
place and time. The text waits,
curled up at the edges, yellowed.
The sunny air is cold, or crisp, as they
say. Meanwhile, I wish you all the best.
See you around in cities, or maybe
right here. Cheers.

The Notebook Troubled The Sleep Door

Morning sound and sure the notebook on my left thigh
The pen is right-handed and translates the windows who
Try to ignore the whole thing, they just stand there agape
At the big new world
Partially over-cast sky enough to stunt the bright therefore
Delivering an everness and a couch that says 'I am not a car'
You would be a door if you could but forming the letters on
The page the goal is an understanding bigger than most, an
Understanding within and beyond understanding a view
Within a view or basically it's about clarity which really is
Quite within and beyond itself, okay, like clean windows or
A morning view
The still driveways of Sunday morning are oily at peace
My tacky Florida coffee mug attempts to follow its own mind
Following thoughts of knowing and not knowing but thoughts
Trying to stay stress-free in spite of the hundred million things to do
And the one day always to do them in, I have to wonder how does
Anyone find time to breathe or at least burp
Hiccup the dream of tomorrow afternoon or just writing what you
Think before you think it, my eyes see and have seen the glory of
The boards coming off the fence or the hoards in their darker
Pursuits but fear not for the coffee table is syrupy brown and is my
Friend in spite of its homogenized Montgomery Wardness
Going out of business a year and half ago clearly a bargain
It was a cheap way to become new again
A seeing way like a toothpaste advertisement

One TV control black with white numbers except the
One red button for what do you suppose an emergency
A hurricane a war or perhaps true silence which
There seems to always be a lack of in fact it doesn't really
Exist but there's my personal phone book fake alligator
Skin black and gold letters in an office-evoking font
At a glance at a marvel telephone miracles and
Addresses both rest on Maya's Chinatown placemat
A Three dimensional vision of fruit, grapes of the original
Grape color like grape ape remember him and strawberries
And there's what looks like a cantaloupe on the outside
Cut in half revealing its insides, an understanding within
An understanding, clarity within and beyond clarity
A clean window a delivered dream which seems
Entirely grapefruit

A grapefruit a juicy fruit a grape ape knocking at the door
A running clumsy looming loony towering over everyone
He also drove a tiny car or rather sat on it clutching his big
Galoot hands on its tiny steering wheel saying like a lunatic
In a deep voice over and over again "Grape Ape, Grape Ape"
Back in the days when cartoons were cartoons, but this is what
I do said the orange to the pear, not wanting to be left out
As fruit I can't identify with the apple in the distance like a
Canadian mountie his conservative red is almost in conflict
With the farmhouse in the background, a blurred harmony
Perhaps of a place one would strive to be, oh how does one begin
A drifting place dream-like though in vivid color I would like

To teach the world to sing I mean live there I mean I am the
World and it would be wonderful to evolve there to arrive
Finally a little acknowledgement or at least some raised eyebrows
Or better yet a simple sincere 'ah' like 'ah, the sky"
It's still morning a new day a minimal place and the
Coffee table by now is hovering in the sturdy lack-light
Of what we're becoming an orange pear a fruit place
A grape ape saving the world from its old face, I bought
Three of them in Chinatown San Francisco in the summer
In one of the many tacky and wonderful souvenir shops
Nestled in the deep quiet, those cold and misty cosmopolitan
Streets, the darkness lit by storefronts streetlights traffic
Lights car lights, take a breath, the stars and moon all slightly
Blurred in this divine sighing this cuddled mist not quite fog
Somehow giving all an ancient depth, what's so funny about
Peace love and understanding within understanding or the
Clarity of I spot a bar called Buddha a red neon fat Buddha
I think to ask Maya to take my picture with it over my shoulder
But decide against it as we already are the gleaming awkward
Tourists with plastic bags calling out to the whole town that
We are not from here but obviously elsewhere fluorescent
Perhaps as though we belong on the moon or at least in suburbia

The morning is the front, a quiet place on the edge of lack-light
Which is home as the notebook huddles in the coffee wake up
Glances the graces of simply noticing and even noticing what's
Noticed like a lack-light within a lack-light, a window within a
Window a window standing akimbo insisting it be taken seriously

Agape at the big new Sunday world with its driveways reluctantly
Smiling in anticipation of Sunday morning's shift into the blunter
Force of afternoon, picking up its traces of children smiling and
Ants constructing fortresses sometimes as the writing continues
The rivers of melancholia break up into what seems like a delta
Where the reeds give life-sustaining forces to the new evolving
Courses, it's an ever-expanding likeness, rivers within rivers
Within rivers, a light within a light a dream a flash a drip
Of night sweat onto the wisteria almost hysterical in its
Expansion, especially in the subtleness of just waking up
And simply transcribing what's there, well of course, it has
To be, how could it not be anything other than everything

NINE RIVER WAYS

1.

The current of the river is slight but full.
It can be called slight only in the most
minimal sense. Like a thin cloth, a cotton
dress, or perhaps cotton candy.

2.

My friend calls me on the phone heart-broken
and dejected. He says he sometimes thinks of
suicide. I do my best to console him. I attempt
to tell him what can't be told, like this will all
pass. The river passes and passes continually.
In this way it never passes.

3.

Tangled in the melancholic vines of the back
porch, the river is a strange companion. Just
when you think you've got it figured out,
it moves on.

4.

The river leads into the bay.
The bay leads into the Gulf of Mexico.
The Gulf of Mexico leads into the Atlantic
Ocean, which is plainly depicted in my
head, as it is on the globe on top of the book
shelf in the dining room.

5.

I think of all the times I've camped on the river's edge. Those memories are far away like distant campfires. The river, however, has stayed in the exact same place, more or less.

6.

Trying to do too much in too little time can expedite suffering, old age, and death. I sip coffee made from river water and take a slow deep breath.

7.

Trying to imitate Wallace Stevens while thinking of the river is good for you. I dreamed of him the other night. I remember his conservative suit and over-all appearance. He was confident, with one foot in the river and one in the world.

8.

Wind nestles the aged pecan trees as well as the elementary cedar. The crows let it blow them around over the manicured cemetery. This seems to be a pleasure for them. They almost seem like black fish being swept along in the river's current.

9.

She dreamt she was made of river water and this meant perfection. She dreamt she walked like a river in human form. Later that morning, over coffee and bagels, when she was describing this to me, I could see it perfectly—a walking river in human form.

Sleepover

No memory of dream
but the smell of onion
I cut last night hitting
me hard like an offensive
wall with reinforcements
as soon as I turned right,
coming down the stairs.

> Nothing is so
> overbearing
> as onion bits
> freshly cut
> left in the
> trash
> overnight.

I say overnight and I see
the little bear wearing pajamas
and a nightcap on his head.
Maybe he's pulling the chain
to a light, as if to say goodnight.
Somewhere one day I'll meet
that little bear, who seems quite
human. Perhaps we'll have some
tea with honey in it. I'll be made
to feel safe in his presence, and
he'll be happy to have my company.
A sleepover in another world.

13 Ways of Looking at a Red-Tailed Hawk

While tiredly walking across the empty college campus,
Begging the shift from academia to mundane perfection
And domestic quietude.

Standing twenty feet under its perch, thinking it's as big as a turkey,
Staring into its two black eyes staring directly at me, ignoring the mocking
Bird nipping at its lower back.

Driving down Davis Highway early in the morning, half asleep, passing
Eighteen-wheelers and contemplating the term *urban sprawl*.

While listening to opera in the company car, Hildegard who
Referred to herself as "A feather on the breath of God."

Thinking of the word *feather* and the word *God*, then thinking of
Gravity and Galileo and noticing the bare feet of the homeless man
Laughing and spinning near the interstate exit.

Thinking of feathers falling and the white feathers on its stocky legs
And remembering how in a dream I once saw a flock of hawks
Moving in formation across the sky.

Sitting in the steam room at the Y with a group of mostly naked
Gay men, thinking I'm probably the only straight guy in here.

While watching stiff academic faces on TV declare who the real Emily
Dickinson was and wasn't, a hawk, a dove, or a poetic man eater with
A monstrous sense of humor.

Walking around a seedy neighborhood with a GPS unit on my back
Seeking timely connections with satellites orbiting the planet and chatting
With wonderfully eccentric trash collectors, also orbiting the planet.

Wanting to slow down wanting to make poetry wanting to do nothing
For God's sake for the sake of nothing for crying out loud and just
Because doing nothing is good for you.

While drinking tea and listening to the washer and dryer noises.

While looking at a picture of Abe Lincoln at a bus stop.

While looking at graffiti on a dumpster that says, "Cops rule, Plants drool,"
Scratching my head, and wondering what that's all about.

lay the dreams
in a pile
the dreams lay
mainly in the pile
the main dreams
are in the pile
a pile driver from
the state of Maine
is a heavy dreamer
like laundry, the
dreams are in a pile
the pile and all its
secrets have a lot
to offer
in the pile of dreams
anything is possible
or so it seems
each dream is its own
place and time, its
own phenomenon
the pile of dreams
sometimes glows,
moves, shifts, and
changes shapes
other times it appears
to be a lifeless heap
of spent energy
and sometimes the
pile simply becomes
invisible and is out
of view
heavy and thick

like a swamp
sometimes no one
dream can be recalled
while the swamp that
is the pile is clearly
recognizable
no two piles are alike
and yet they are all
together the same
where-did-it-go
stuff, nonmaterial
of where, how
and why
which is perhaps
the greatest key of
all, the why key
as the main key
in the life of dreams
in the funk of swamps
to the piles, however,
a resolution or answer
is hardly the point
in fact, it's not
the point at all
why, like clouds
is the humble
active firecracker
which is a key
which is a look
which is a balloon
stuck high in a tree
mostly forgotten

and simply seen
as just a balloon
stuck high in a tree
and nothing more
much like a pair
of tennis shoes
tied together
hanging on
a telephone wire
or shopping carts
randomly left
anywhere
out in the world
street corners
vacant lots
sidewalks
and schoolyards
why, not the
question, but the
statement
why as a statement
not a question
continuity of why
as everything, I stand
before you
in why
baptized
in the waters
of why
there goes the fool
and all his whys
why be born

why die
why live
why the lights on
why the lights off
why make the bed
why write poetry
why did the chicken
cross the road
to get across
you fool
or why did the
utility truck squash
the chicken, splat
gocsh, scattering
feathers randomly
everywhere
because it is a utility
truck in the heat
and brutality that
is the surface
of the scene
the feathers fly
like the shopping carts
the shoes on the line
the balloon bouncing
alone, maybe black
maybe blue maybe red
squish goes the chicken
and the feathers fly
and the utility truck
will drive on for
what seems like

a long time
with what seems
to be little
or no remorse
for the chicken
until it runs out of
gas, reaches its
end, is retired
and stripped of its
parts, a rusted metal
hunk in some junkyard
and like the feathers
most anywhere
and anywhere is why
and somewhere
is anywhere
and maybe the driver
of the utility truck
kept driving
and perhaps said
"damn" or maybe
even "got em"
and never thought
about it again
maybe that night
she dreamed of
the chicken
maybe she pulled
off to the side
of the road
got out of the truck
and went to the

chicken, maybe she
was hurt and remorseful
and moved
the chicken's body
off the road
muttered a prayer
and apologized
greater still, she takes
one of the scattered
feathers and lays it
on her bedside table
later that night
the why clouds and
the why clear blue sky
the pile of dreams lays
in the corner
by the refrigerator
by the stereo
in the middle of the
room by nothing
the feather, blown
off the table, floats
to the floor, tiny
in its descent
the gravity of what
things become
in an eye blink
no difference
in anything
in an eye blink
absolute difference
in everything

in an eye blink
the world on our
shoulders
in an eye blink
we carry the weight
of the world
hum the song of
the weight of the
world
the humming
of the dream piles
humming
of the fields
of the discarded
shopping cart
dislodged of its
purpose, momentarily
out of the linear
loop, finally outside
of predictability
listen to its new speech
listen as it discovers
its own tongue
its life force
and soft decay
the dreams are
piled over there
the dreams
are piled right here
the pile of dreams
is glowing and blinking
its eyes, the changing

eyes of dreams
the chance music
of the piles
the dreams lay
mainly in the pile
the piles wash
over themselves
to become waves
the waves become
fences, the fences
become bicycles
the bicycles become
clotheslines that become
vast cities with millions
of people, car lights
windows and noises
the cities become dying
creeks that become
vacant lots
the dream piles
chuckle in the middle
of the room
the room is a woodpile
burning
the pile of dreams
is smoke on the
beach in winter
blending
with stars
one more star in
the program
one more moon

in the backseat
one more grain
of sand in my ear
one more buoy
one more bell
ringing across the
water, one more smile
on the face
of unknowing
on the face of why
as a kingdom, a key
a hidden city
a marble
the piles return
to thin air, go back
to the same sky
air, same why material
why is a letter
and you should
know better
why is a word
like a bird
in the day world
born from the
dream piles
placed, misplaced
alone together
lay the dreams
in the pile
the dreams lay
mainly in
the pile

IF YOU SEE AN OCELOT, PLEASE REMOVE THIS LETTER

(2006-2007)

Sunrise the cold front
Grey morning Sunday steering
Me where but tumbling like
The Sweetgum leaves in the
Front yard yellow in the
Drift the shift the blue
Music of back to basics
And standing straight no
Shame in the frame of
Who you are
                    Because
At their most basic the spaces
Fill themselves in even
And perhaps especially on
Sunday barely awake though
Fully ourselves this being
Before Sunday's sticky mirror
Tricks begin disconnecting
A from B and head from toe
Before one assumes the
Burdens it is here at this
Early grey space quiet
That the past says nothing and
Sits somewhat disconnected
Head down but never discontinued
Or far away from the fray
                    Because
The stern face of the
Woman in the vine, the
One not connected to the
Earth, stares down on me
From within her undulating
Tentacles. Perhaps that is why
She seemed deeply sad, while

Her other half, fully rooted,
Was composed and calm, smiling,
Lit up, and gracious
                          Because
Last night I was a cop
Without a gun, and I didn't
Know how to work my siren
Or blue light, and I could
Never seem to make it to
The neighborhood crime I was
Called to, I kept getting
Distracted and taking wrong
Turns, and my mother was
Worried sick
                          Because
I'll gladly assume the sign
That some people should be
Cops and some, clearly,
Should not
                          Or sunlight
Then, a phone call good morning
So sweet as if light were more
Than light, which it is I'm sure
As if everything sensed on
The outside extends inside
As well, which, yes, it must,
Of course
                          So delivering the
News so sorry of good
Morning then is delivered
Again now even though
This morning is grey
So experience blends the
Sleepy-headed past delivers

And I have no memory
Then of the alarm going
Off but this morning did
And do but even more
So the train horn around
7:30 continued an extra
Long time, waking me, causing
Me to notice, and suspect
The worst, a person
Or car on the tracks,
Or some train conductor
Playing a joke, "Fuck it,
If I have to be out this
Early then everybody else
Can wake the fuck up!"
Shower brewed the basics
Sunlight coffee arise
There are young poets and
Trees and dreams to
Scribble—doughnuts to
Unearth and new earths
Awaiting
              Thinking of
The attic again I think
Of the stars thinking of
The stars I think of
Infinite space thinking of
Infinite space I think of
Heaven thinking of heaven
I think of no place in particular
But back to the window
Of gray Sunday turning
Lighter, timely shift of the
Thought of morning and

Coffee and poems and it's
Hard not to smile if only
A little.

Season's Greetings

for Jack Collom and Jennifer Heath

Dear Jack and Jenny, your merry Christmas O holy night iron collection erect on the shelves of a sunny cool morning sure does flourish in my mind like a rare gem possibly red but maybe blue and certainly happy as any other season too! One strong frog centers this dream, a cold glinting metal sculpted in the same morning light as the irons gone on strike. But friends are friends let's begin in the most upper left corner a lit flashed ghostly clothes hanger of a thing, or rabbit ear related antennae for falling behind TV somewhere stranded 30 or 40 years back last century, it's a ghostly corner though quite connected to a light source to be sure. Beside the sundown second story porch of a sky burning orange and the code of dark treescapes of stories almost spooky but only because it's not so small as the mall in the mind's own field, not predictably safe and restrained but quite untamed and as wild as any strip of sky haze in the shift adrift at the end of any long gone day. A strip of pool ladder lies therein, a middle day or morning born into or perhaps a bleacher but no, a one two three step brown and barely a fourth a pool in my head gone to sleep, all waterless and white. The dark pulls it in like life, turns smoothly to cobalt blue two bars two strips a soothing right of horizontal a sigh a grounding ok. Spray-painted red circle on a slate with a black-line x a cross and a circle inside—a head a dream a stick figure a marked spot hello as if nearly the gray grain could be wood or cinderblock cement asbestos shingle as canvas red as in the heat intensity circular and plain to see yes by a reflecting window right corner once again the horizontal lines figure our sensibilities into the scope though this time black tan brown gray off-white hazy gray blue reflection as if floating as if in a new light for another, much other, corner. Below she red-lipped and white crème high cheeks defined in full swiftly stares ahead, a strawberry in the floated force field of everything about the girl is simply terrific streamlined in the mannequined morning of intimate distance of window reflection o joy the trees the lights blue sky space time darkness.

Hovering, the strawberry makes it simple sweet seemingly misplaced yet balanced on a ghostly line of light, it lowers the wild imaginings in my head, a grounding force at the base of her Billy Blake halo—her vogue black strands and lips perfected slip forward yet sideways like dreams of space making perfect strawberry sense milked and spliced into what in the hell is that jack and jenny? A green embryo of a thing, a reindeer or a bird dinosaur mutant kangaroo ostrich whippet iguana??! Seemingly on a paper plate for goodness sakes! The bottom half of strawberry elegance round with toenails and a beak underneath her chic lovely light. Science glimpses itself in the darnedest of places strips of street life night day the sidewalk might as well lead straight off the planet lest we forego our silly hats of humor and sink into tree rings, unable to say 'Hey, wouldja' look at that,' 'Wow,' and/or 'Holy shit motherfuck whaddya' know!' Street lamp base ringed on dark curb brown leaf particles littered before the lighter brighter street extends out. Another piece looking like a sci-fi beach of mars if mars had blue with orange fire lights and black trees a painting a book cover a dream in the hurried nuance of a keen awareness of a somewhere else—these two strips somehow hopeful displayed laid dropped landed on the cement street parking lot playground ball court bottom right corner an arrow, white, points back into the flux, keeping us inside, guiding our attention, not allowing us to stray completely off the page white arrow headed northwestward saving us bringing us fourth and back toward our nucleus hero sculpted frog whose energy on the cold earth is timeless and in fact suggestive of all good once and future frogs, and hope in water and water in hope, stick your head out of any rainy window and breathe, friend, letting your primal ooze wash away in a beautiful rain she might even be an Aztec frog timely and strong staring up into the heavens but back to the arrow white on asphalt it contains a red spot circle soft red almost nearly valentine red red circle in white arrow defining nothing or anything aimed at the Aztec amphibian and the noble and dignified gathering of irons but underneath it a wing perhaps of a hawk or is it a pineapple or some other fantastically shamanistic coconut I must be losing it says the Christmas recipient by now but hark hold on! There are leaves there are leaves there are leaves in fall-like lesser shades of red auburn yellow gold peach blended still on the branches I imagine air and wind straight up easy breathing (sigh) and oxygen quite clearly a nice tree in a subtle camp of earth somewhere triangular photos of a Joshua tree gray backdrop starkly contrasting our fall thanksgivings anywhere a new difference and the strips of brown of perhaps our earlier prehistory swimming pool steps although now they are something entirely different, clues to steps of ladders brown that might be shelves for all we know one seems to have an oval shape but only a strip of this, of this photographic glue of bits of pieces slices of time stitched pasted in the gathered moments of a friendly and hospitable milieu, still laid in the leaves in the layered left corner under the ever-proud and upright irons we greet merry xmas and merry xmas happy new year back at ya true dat folk!

11:40

At peace a plane dips dives
sleeps late
        Society comes back
to life people do their jobs
A good ride at Christmas tree
A flat feeling incredibly mellow
but for the worm-like uneasiness
of being alone
Morning nearly gone but still
here
        Slept till gone 11 what in
the world? The bed the bed
the bed felt good. Dream filled
though I can't recall any of
them at the moment.
            Fred leaves
a message earlier informing me
that "my reality check bounced
(that's a funny joke)" and that he
won't be able to help me in the
garden, that's ok, he already
has a house so quite apart from
the coffee pot crinkle and the
airplane ruffle rumble up and
down sound.

Trying to recall how the soles
of a specific pair of boots
got partially melted. Going through
an old box of clothes the other
day I find them, redwings, leather,
I remembered them pretty well.

Not much support but otherwise
tough durable and fairly cool
looking. When I pull them from
the box, I notice the sole of each
shoe is partially gooey, each has
a portion that is literally gooey.
My hands get stained and sticky
from touching them—this after
two years in a box—as best I
recall, that happened when I put
my feet too close to a fire for
too long. I believe it was at
the beach blanket pipe bomb
extravaganza—*this bike is a
pipe bomb* played at the trestle—
me and Scotty, drunk as drunk,
closed the place down, the last
two standing, or rather, stumbling,
everybody gone but us, Scotty
peeing on the smoldering remains
of the fire, me, sitting in the sand
with my melted boots.

11:04

butterflies, a corona of
butterflies surround my head,
they are blue, it is no
dream it is marcus saying
a marcus lovely thing from
san diego over the foggy
phone line where I waking
from nearly noontime sleep-late
receive it well

THE DESTROYED ROOM
for Phyllis

the shins were alive
and at least one student
wrote
my friend, now six years
dead, visits me in dream
says she never died
her smile was beautiful
beer on the notebook
fog outside the door
new music and new
gardens to live by
but I swear, as much
as I want it, I run
from new love
I'm a comet coming apart
and buffalo occupy my
dreams
tonight the saints
win and we are endeared
to them
running from love
and running in time

I want to smoke because
I love the idea of it
not death and cancer
but a smoky vice
a beautiful train sound
somehow fully transferred
through the smoky humid
fog, a damp song, and

love is gone, a damp
dream of here it is and
what are we passing

passing ships
passing parades
your smile was so
good last night,
I'm glad you came,
or I came, glad we met
in the unframed frame
land of dream
and now in dreams it
means everything
a one at a time
time frame

the teacher dreams
a thousand new songs
but doesn't get them
out before they shift
before they pass but life
so suddenly becomes more
becomes less becomes
eloquently unfamiliar
as in a million minute
slivers fall into place
and if only in your
head, there appears
to be reason to smile.

January 27, 2007
for Bernadette and Phil

Your poem is inspiring
It is a night trick of a Wednesday
A mushroom on the dirty range
It flowers in my mind now like
A trickling stream and like the
Yellow paper upon which it is
Printed, I've fallen under its spell,
Having only read it once, with its
Flowering endearments of democracy
And governor runners made of snow,
It is certainly a smiling poem, and
thank goodness for that! Your poem
Is inspiring as I aspire to flower in the
Way up way it speaks of freedom,
Freely forming like bright yellow
Paper or the tiny yellow flowers
Starting to dart the yard, practically
Popping up everywhere, by force or
By delirious weather, meteorological
Tomfoolery, of which we are all
Participants and products of these
Days, and this is nothing new really
But it is a new year, and your new-
Year poem is inspiring, a first-time
Delight, now having been read twice,
Make that thrice, to where morel is
Swell in almost any language, like
The French morille, or even the Dutch
Morilijet, which might clumsily
Rhyme with I don't know how to
Say, or see, but probably not, though

I think of John Cage, who I'm sure
Would know, and even if he didn't
That would be ok, or what about
The Welsh morel, the Czech, or the
Finnish? Let's call Anselm Hollo
He'd probably know, and even if he
Didn't we'd still be free to choose,
Like the new 2007, as mentioned in
Your mostly yellow poem, which is
Nothing like the government but
Certainly utopian, if it were a shirt
I'd happily wear it, or a hat, scarf,
Or any other piece of clothing, but
It's not, so I'll put it back on the
Refrigerator for now and read it
Once a day or more, or not, or
Perhaps just look at it, a glancing
Shift, a drifting yellow knowing,
As I go glowing most mornings with
Coffee, laundry, sleepy lunchbox
Thoughts and water bottle refills
So inspired I am by its hints of new
Beginnings and borderless imaginings,
I lightly lend it forward and lean
Into its future, a day in the life of
your mostly yellow poem

LOOK POSSIBLE
for Dylan

I'm looking possible.
I'm on the refrigerator
smiling a crisp and somewhat
strained 6-year-old smile.
I'm on there twice actually.
I'm also sitting by a snowman
and some presents.
Everything's white like the
movie *Elf*, and I could
be the snowman's brother.
My eyes are coal-black like his,
and my calm demeanor is as close
to his as possible for a boy who's
made of flesh and bone, not snow.
I'm looking possible you can see
me if you try.
Two possible boys on the
refrigerator, with one possible
snowman.
Everything possible is in my
look, like a boy without the
hint of any such idea, which
is precisely what's required
for this and any possible world,
for I am on the refrigerator
looking possible, as possible
as can be.
To look possible I am smiling
gently. My smile is almost
like a cool stick I picked
up in my backyard,
but not quite.

My other smile, there are
two you know, is a black line,
also not unlike a stick but this
time not from the backyard
but probably from the charred
remains of a really great campfire,
because campfires are really
cool and seem to make everything
possible, like my little smile,
which is anything but confusion,
it simply lays there across my
face like a stick.

This burnt-stick smile matches
my black eyes, which are like
two pieces of coal, as are my
snowman brother's.
I'm looking possible sitting
quaintly on a box waiting
for Santa and for my picture
to be done with. I am posing
possibly in the way that even
though I am posing my pose
suggests the possibility that
the boys, namely me and me,
and the snowman can be brothers,
and even friends, which is certainly
a reason to smile, which is clearly
a reason to pose politely twice
on the refrigerator, which is
as good of a reason as any to
look as possible as a I can,
which is exactly what I'm
doing.

YO LA TANGO

smoke seems like steam
steam delivers a golden sun
rooftops glisten
morning's new guitar sounds
but only in the rounded seconds
of earth's massive turn
it's then I yearn, more hardy
than wishes, than the toughest
of fishes, swimming upstream
in some freeway ravine

Because You Are Pisces

for Llisa

1

because you are Pisces, my
world has always had an
unrestricted quality to it,
a left-handed blueishness perhaps,
or purple or green gone pink—
suffice to say that because
you are Pisces I've had living
proof that there's always
another way, an option to
what *they* say, so much more
than the day-to-day so
dreary and dry, a trap
screen-door to a star-lit
sky—always something kooky
and fun, like a clown galloping
along on a make-believe horse,
singing all night, and poetry
of course!

2

because you are Pisces, new
music arrives in bundles and
Chucky was in love and probably
still is, and Rickie Lee wore a
beret (was it red?) and looked
broken and flawed and
beautiful, smoking and smiling and
leaning toward a deeper meaning
of things, like the grey
morning rain—because you
are Pisces I am Aries and
the science of stars and living
light make it possible to
smile, that's our style.

3

because you are Pisces, I not only
know what being "vaccinated with a
victrola needle" means, I take it
to heart, i.e. it's personal, and
personally endearing—a type of
spiritual 'medal of honor' bestowed
on my sister by God by stars
by heaven by the glue that
binds us true, and therefore
connected to my hip my heart my
art, constantly providing me with
another view, allowing me the
grace to see past time and space—
and the heroic simplicity of tricycles,
or the outrageousness of an
ape-man harassing kids in a
volkswagon toward the end of a
darkening blue decade quickly
closing down.

4

because you are Pisces I
remember colorfully painted
mailboxes. the sun's golden
shafts, fringed leather jackets
with hippy patches, latches
to lighters, rolling papers.
because you are Pisces Nana
kept rainwater in a barrel, a
drum, on the carport where the
sun might nearly warm it by mid-
afternoon but not quite—it was
always so perfectly cold and
clear—I can still see it, and
feel it, jiggly mosquito larvae
and all, and because you are
Pisces I am there now, thinking
of renewal. joy, and familial love.

5

because you are Pisces I lay
sleeping, blanketed by a 1930's
white light, soft and angelic, a
cigar in my mouth, bespectacled like
Groucho Marx I am dreaming of other
worlds, calm, beautiful, and absurd
worlds because you are Pisces
and the pieces fit beyond
themselves, connecting to the
seemingly unfilled spaces, relegated,
unweighted, extended out and
within a never-ending story, and
because you are Pisces I remember
Nana napping, fully clothed,
eye-glasses in one hand, pink fleshy
indentations where they'd sat on
her nose, a little breathing body,
tiny worker of God, in heaven,
Amen.

6

because you are Pisces we sometimes
sense the oddest glimpses, as if we
were dreaming people elsewhere
in a far-corner Europe of our
heads, and because you are
Pisces, of the equatorial region
of the northern hemisphere,
holding near, mere stellar neighbor
to Aries and Pegasus, 12th sign of
the zodiac, also called "Fish" or
"Fishes," and because of this I've
known fish in a different way—
some people are people and some
people are Pisces people, and
you are one of them, and I am
with you, which gets me in,
through the door, so to speak,
like saying, "I'm with the band,"
except the band is a fish made
of stars, heavenly molded as my
sister, folded in the grace of
late-night skies, when others
are sleeping you shine—born
under the sign.

RECLAIMING THE WINDOW

for Eileen Myles

the Christmas tree kidnapped
the window
or instead
we pick up the light
of Eileen's *Sorry, Tree*
and say see ya' later alligator,
or greetings to all of you
of this Sunday morning spring
where ever new, the dogwoods
blossom white green whispers
elegant azaleas swoosh pink
into bird talk sunlight

two doves upon waking
I will read Eileen
and drink windows
I will be the perfect poet,
perfectly flawed by windows
I wake up writing this poem,
to you, the every part of me
that's always smiling.

NEW SPRING

dear rainy day
there are a million
and one places to begin
as the light tap of drizzle
sustains itself into ever
lighter and heavier rolls
a squirrel slowly and carefully
works his way up the
sweetgum tree
a mockingbird hops
in flight before my eyes
at least one mosquito has bitten
the inside of my right ankle
the same mockingbird flies
past again (in the opposite
direction) but this time with
a twig in its beak
taking it to the shrub by
the neighbor's driveway
where he could possibly
be building a nest
I am slightly hung-over
in wine town today
where the leftover prattle
of last night's dinner still
fuses in my head
everyone seemed to speak
in fragments
at times simultaneously
and it seemed like a
competition to get a word

in edgewise
I sat on the edge of the
porch of what used to be
my home
a silent gargoyle
in need of air
amid the crazed domestic
swirl of my little family
the competitors spoke
loudly and quickly
disinterested in following
any thought through
an idea
a statement to top the
last thing said by
themselves
a continuous chopped
conversation
but the sunshine of the
etouffee was exquisite
and the red wine was
good
much like your rain
at present
unaffected by the
familial loose ends
wind and falling leaves
too many various bird
calls to count
I stop for the
need to be slow
I Tibetan prayer flag

my dream-like perennials
and slip softly
and quietly
into April.

Freeing The Stamps

Swimming in the
Dishwater
I did my bills
Or they did me
Easter wind
Lifts us up
To begin
A Saturday of
Kind sleep
The weather
In my vane of
Heads
Softly treads

Calzaghe

Easter Wind
awake
fingers hands cold
the last of winter's
overtones
Maya and I discuss
spirituality this morning
in our pajamas
typically uncomfortable
discussion
she doesn't understand
why it's important to
discuss this
"so you can understand
what it means to me,"
I say.

Last night we attempt
to watch *The Lake House*,
but couldn't make it past
the mailbox flag continually
rising by itself
we lasted ten minutes
maybe

That was after we
rooted for the Welsh
boxer to defeat the
American boxer
so glad we were to
see Wales on TV
watching the crowd in

Cardiff go nuts when
the Welsh national
anthem is sung, in
Welsh, of course

Sunrise service ruled-
out by sleep
alarm clock turned off
barely a memory
dove in her nest
feathers fluffed
in palm tree
outside my bedroom
window
"Poetry can be so
many more things
than what people
mostly believe it
is."
　　Anslem Hollo

The World of Magazines

dogs bark troubled birds
leathery days Saturday
everyone wants
communal
bliss
new morning friends
hit the road
having stayed overnight
long enough to bring light
to old memory strands
and altogether forgotten
experiences
transfiguration of
the morning
leaves me
bumbling
into
a forward
future
stance
ghost handwriting be done
poet in the cupboard
Indian in the head dream
alligator in the heart stream
sliding forward, in slow
motion, purposeful,
driven, timely.

MORNING POCKETS

ready or not
not a Texaco
nor a Mexico
but a dream
of a double
double image
free
desert
mars
heal   cold   blue

here I am with my
heart in my hand
blue before sunrise,
I wait for no one
crinkled lightly my suit
of waves skitters into
cartoon frequencies
    lone frog in the
morning lost
      not lost but lingering
letting us in on the
coming of rain

a ship in a painting
a fatherly tie from
a blue place of water
blurred life where time
dives deep floating to
where all roads stop
top
    of

              a planet
way up in a head
plurality in all its
expansiveness

the strands go brown
they are blowing
backwards into what
time has done slipped
freely but with
a weightless
forcefulness
all its own
skeletons dancing
in place
morning parade

VICTORIAN

Picture-perfect house,
Victorian. Clean, ancient
Wood. Not a museum
But more like a picture
Available in some student's
Book-bag. Someone owns
This house, as if it were
A school supply. This
House is picture-perfect
Victorian school supplies.
It is a picture that can be
Stepped into at any time.
In this way you can carry
Your home in your
Book-bag. A ready-made
Home. Not a home but a
Photo-shoot. We might
Live here but probably
Do not but we will
Pose for our family
Photograph here.
Victorian. Once
The home of Louis
Armstrong. Now it is
A photograph school
Supply ready-made
Place to pose. We see
Old photos of it from
When Louis was a
Child. It is quite
Different now. Less
Buildings around it.

More of a single house
Surrounded by space
As opposed to being
Tightly enclosed by
Other houses.
In time, it grew free.
In time it earned, or
Developed, space.
Earning space one
Dream at a time.
Like developing
Photographs, our
Realities are carried
As school supplies in
Our book bags.
A home whenever
We need it.
A photograph space
Ready to step into.
A place to pose,
Unburdened for yet
Another photograph.
Victorian.

morning
to write by
be reborn by
to blow by blow
rejuvenate
glow up out extend
into the day's timed
array of 8 classes
if only in the sense
of smiling
I am not a doctor
nor a subordinate
in some doomed
sense of order
but then again
perhaps then again
just maybe then again
I'll just swing low
on second thought
I'll build my days
in crayon book moments
of sky patterns seen
and unseen
of the miraculous order
of the termites
swarming
out of two sides
of the sweet gum tree
at dusk, when the day
becomes a tent
of evening, breezes
scattering winged ants

amid the stars
and buzzing
streetlight
silences

reflective in morning
last night I thought of
all the silence that
accompanies, surrounds
each thought in my
head, the vast silence
of every thought
sitting still on the dock,
occasional star glint
bending, rocking
train rumble
the dark distant cars
on the bridge
little minnows flashing
beneath my
dangling
feet

into it we lift
into it we softly slip
as if no one ever
knew, as if we
never knew

TELESCOPE

(2002-2010)

"helping salt be born"

heaven and grand street
leaves do somersaults through
the air over my backyard

had a dream the other night
that I was with Robert Creeley
and he was trying on new
eyes
that is new single eyes for
his one empty socket
some made him look like pop music
some more feminine and mall-like
others made him look pink and
as though he should work in a
Hallmark card shop
all of them made him seem
most unlike who he was, Robert
Creeley, so he chose none,
and remained himself.

Under The Big Span of Small Regards

When there's orange things in the tuna,
be scared.

When the moon is fully eclipsed and
the little criminal walking behind your
house with a flashlight hauls off and
kicks your fence, let him.

The stain on the moon is red
and your life is short.

New books are born all the time
and people die just the same.

Did the blackbirds in the roof see
the eclipse, and if so what did they
think? Did they feel it?

All the people walk out slowly in
their driveways and yards and look
up at the moon. They point to the sky
and calmly chat their observations
to one another. Others sit on the hoods
of their parked cars a few feet off of
the busy highway and look as though
they're in a tranquil forest, staring
upward.

The vanishing world misplaces itself
in these darker minutes of Thursday.
The science of love and loss are not
reversed, but somehow seem diluted,
at least temporarily.

SWIMMING

"And so when any day one might
need life and help from others of the
working poor, there was no way a
woman who had a little saved could
say them no."

Gertrude Stein, 3 Lives

Could say them no. Could tell
them no. Could refuse them.
Could turn them down. Could
deny them.
    Could imply the
bridges before them. Could
say them no in their going.
Could go fourth into wind-filled
denial. Could fly into the force
of refusal. Could lift up, suddenly,
like a torn black plastic trash
bag and be carried over the
bayou where the peaceful nutria
swim and rest. Could say them
no in a subtle going. Could go
in the no-like ways of
fearfulness.
    Could be nearer to
light than fear. Could say them
no in regards to the moths
hungrily flying into the light.
Who could refuse them? Could
say them no to the fear
before them and thus
restore them.

Could zip fourth the
weathered sidewalk's tropical
aromatic ooze. Could say them
no in fierce lightening. Under
doorways and awnings. Who
could deny them shelter from
the ridiculously monsoon-like
rain? Could say them softly.
Could lightning crack at their feet
and on their heads they would
have no chance to say no.
Could say them no to the kind
proprietor who brought them white
hand towels draped over his
forearms for them to dry with.
Could softly fold them. Could
softly reminisce navigational
denial and the light of friendship.
Could say them no. So slight of
going. Going on. Could say
them onward where style is
done. Like bridges or boats
or rediscovered booking agents.
These are the horse days.
Who could deny them. Could
flat refuse them.
                   Many say
no to the nutria. Their glow
is much too rat-like, which
arouses instant fear and aversion.
Could say them and do. Could
fear them in an utmost way that
certainly bypasses reason. Could
bend before them as to ignore

them but they're way too
visible for that. Could say
them no like some bayou
sharpshooters. Four bucks a pop.
Four bucks paid by the state of
Louisiana for every nutria tail.
Four bucks a tail. Could fear them.
The tail is what gets them in
trouble. It's a tail like a snake.
It's a slithering tail. Could say them
no. Were it more like a squirrel's
tail they might be off the hook.
The bayous are full of them. They
sleep in the day and play at night.
They are not fools but the
fearful foolish say them
no and loudly.
         Could say
them no in wind blowing.
No before not but not without
knowing. Simply seeing is
beginning. Which is nowhere
near no. A no knock at the door.
Delicious. Superfluous. Outrageous.
Could say them no in power
outages. Where grace by
darkness. Who could bend
them. Beyond the telephone.
Could say them yes with
subtle glances. A subtle
saying them.
         Some go saying
in nutria fur jackets. Saying
them no but stealing their

fur. Skinning nutria for no-like
reasons. For warmth and fashion.
For them who wear the rodent
proudly. Could say them no. In
plastic pockets windy blowing.
Could say for a second flying nutria
imagined. Imaginary sayings of
proverbial denial. Could flat
refuse them. Or bind them
lightly within monsoon images.
None too soon could say them
shivering. Or working their way
straight into the light. Even
within the tackling foreboding.
One goes. One stays. One sips
the savage moments of movie-set
rains. Could say them desirable
moments less leaning them some.
Some streetcars seem less. Less
leaning in the Stella screaming
pouring. Could deny them the
downpour. Could purr in their
taken wet streets.

              Could say
them no what working poor
could wonder. Could instill some
light from far off sources.
One has to wonder. What
distances said might decrease
by saying. More bridges. Who
could say them no. Who could
no say them. Who could them
say no by such simple sounding.
The nearer numbers of rainstorms.

Too timely by clouds. Timely
enough not urgent and then some.
Could say them no. At little to no
cost. What is the cost of
kinship. Friendship slips could
say them further. A further
saying in some way sayable.
Who could say them no is
a promise to light candles
or a conversation about god.
The godly and lowly. The
lowly and the blow floats.
I would hesitate your numbers
to say them yes in navigational
instances. A lighter of candles
in the deep lush hollers. Could
say them no in mountain
neighborhoods. Hoodwinked in
saying, some move forward
in the best sense of boards.
Going forward like boards
becoming and anything
but boring.
            Could say them
no in their going forth. Like
boards like stars or stairs to
a perfect instance. To say
them no in traffic rallying
onward released as song
so long so going.

TELESCOPE

fences diminish, crumble, fall
while landscapes reminisce about
old loves
earth afloat in the mote of time
and space, surrounded by books
in the afternoon, awash in Saturday's
vast white smile, mile after mile
the meals add up, expand, nourish,
and disappear, save us the truth
that makes us shine
curiosity the wine of this new
light, morning, month, year,
decade, and score, more big bang
for the slang machine, more oil
for the hinges on the door of
I hear voices, train horns, and
thunder, or could it be a plane
way off in the corner
write a note to a star some
slippery morning
write letters to the dead on any
given Friday
cradle the shifts, the transitions,
the cruxes, the latter-day
evolutions, and revolutions of what
the dust does at night, cemetery
quietude be blessed
just as books move beyond
themselves upon being opened
and read, the hero's first step
is to get out of bed, or not
everything happening for no

reason at all in the big fields
of reason, where the seasons
extend one into the other, and
every minor part is part of
every major other, and timing,
as it turns out, is indeed
understandably relevant,
pertinent to our multiple dips
in the lake, swims in the river,
tumbles in the eddies
and this is the deal this afternoon,
a few minutes past four, cartooned
maneuvers and breath works
of riding-out Saturday,
parking lot clouds drift in
massive bulks between the
church and the bookstore,
leaving everyone in a damp
state of contentment
barking from the womb, we
push forward onto the streets,
where the earth and sky continue
to clatter and clang
scattering, we go our myriad ways
amid the flotsam and jetsam, to be
washed in with the tide of
Saturday's white futures,
unspoken in the turbulent swish,
delicate, clear, and tinted by
a tiny but definite sense of
smiling.

FIRST HAND

for Keith Waldrop

And so the single dromedary,
appearing from the page
into a fuller field of mind,
signals choices and
is at once disabling
and empowering,
variably (like an idea of
God that holds water, but
is in no way exclusive)
outside of the standard
notions of time, he is
a switch-foot signal of
displacement, more like
a mood than a mammal

Just as Buckminster Fuller
referred to God as a verb,
this static image-turned-idea
continues to turn, much
like the weather or the
day chasing night, which
really is no chase at all

the most active sense
perception flitted before
one's eyes, spread out over
tables before what's lovingly
immersed in the stars,
connoting the vast harmonic
identity of every left leaning
sound wave, ripple, *reordering*

of the universe in the guise
of afternoon, Sunday where
lovely is the rain pouring
out-of-doors *from unleashed*
chaos of each passerby
shuffling past our table,
all tight *energy* wound
together by days and pain
and boredom and tears,
adrift in the cradle roll flux
of *whatever words come*
meddling.

                    with lines from Keith Waldrop

Snow Knowing
for Anne Waldman

but in the morning secret planes fly by
limbs as bridges lift reach angular
Balzac shifts from balustrade to nightshade
to street corner myth
shouting absurdities station to station
relation in real-time
a reeling coalescence, subversive coherence
over six lanes of traffic, scattered erratic
dear dearest damage control
I forewarn you
draw in my forces
erect my walls to knock them down
by force by sham by disobedient slight of hand
lingering strands, punctuated filiations
forego foregone strictly foraged
what's left in the dirt, roadside, ditch
pitched songs on walls carved painted
hummed muttered
and this will be nothing and nothing
will be something
and something will shine heraldic incipient
mingled without a language
like Mesopotamia locked inside
there are neurons in the heart, the heart is radiant
the radiance is forever
dynamite delicate full of moon and water
piss and vinegar
saline stretches
lipped across seascapes
buzzed along beaches through deserts cities
continental cosmopolitan

war-zones death trips star shutters
primordial pre-lexical
a dog on a leash systematically sniffs
a cold patch of urban dirt
squared by a sidewalk, steeped in a timing
a nighttime evolution
essentially showered venerated dreamed amphibious
calculating wastelands, speaking paranoia ex-memoria
I implore you, adore you
furtive, suspicious, covered in dirt
stars, leaves, limbs
vulnerable, reluctant
radiant.

TERMINAL

adjust,   bacillus,   colony
cool methods of adapting with grace, back-bend,
shape shift, amongst the green islands of breezes,
waves currents breakers awash tread water
transcendental now and then, before, after, sand,
quartz, washed down from Appalachia, Allegheny,
a blanket a belonging the songs seep, drip, stream
through psychic fractures of age
and location

hope, hone, honor, honorific
signify in place the pacing adjust adapt
to new, new gentle edge, day, afternoon
soft white singing who are we belonging
alone and of morning
god good goddess
geode agate

his eyes are trophy agates   staring up, out from the river bottom

DESOTO
1507

I've never seen a ghost, and tonight I can't sleep.
The sweeping passage of enough time can make
one start to feel like an echo in a can, a moving
shape in a past filling in, but always open.

Tiny
streams
roadside gutters
stick races in the rain

Maya and I walking for
blocks and blocks following
the downward slant of East Hill
streets, observing the path of our floating
sticks as they drift down Desoto, turn left on
16th Avenue, right on Gonzalez and down
past Bill's park, Toledo Square, over
18th,19th, 20th, to the dead end and
disappearing into a culvert that
will spit them into Bayou
Texar, which leads
to Pensacola Bay
which opens
into the
Gulf
of
Mexico

I've never seen a ghost, but my sister sees them often.

Things didn't make sense to me for a long time.
Some sort of fear that was always present,
though of what exactly I don't know.
Of being so small in such a big world,
I think. So small in such vast space.
Feeling fragile within my own skin.

I remember the particles singing one morning while driving
along the bay, to work, City Hall, and thinking, this is what poems
should do.

I remember feeling at peace and nearly perfect sitting against
the sun lit, east brick wall, morning break, coffee, notebook,
and whatever book I was reading at that time. *Maxfield Parrish*

by Eileen Myles, "The Poet," *I made myself into a poet because it was the first thing I really loved.*

I wrote a poem about the color purple.
I don't remember its words, but I clearly recall its power, how sane,
and perfectly placed it made me feel.
I wrote another called "A Lesson in Adjectives," for my friend
and boss, Phyllis. Something about a white room and how it made
me feel to be in it, inspired by some type of personality test she'd given me.
Phyllis, who later died of cancer, and whose eulogy I gave—a poem-talk
comparing her to the Tasmanian devil and Pooh Bear. I was a printer
and for about ten years my hands were always ink stained.
On the day I quit I drove straight from work to her grave, where I placed
a small bouquet of purple flowers, talked to her, thanked her for being my
friend, cried, read new poems, felt silly, profound, and on track. Her last words
to me about our workplace: "You need to get out of here." Resigning was an
effort to take poetry in a different direction, to let it take me, to follow its call.

I have never seen a ghost, but I feel their presence on most days.

Listening to Sun Ra's "Cosmic Tones for Mental Therapy" late one night,
sitting by an open window through which I could hear a mocking bird
aggressively blowing streams of sounds into the neighborhood silence.
I remember a point where both the music and the bird notes began to merge,
synchronize, and riff off of one another. I wasn't even stoned. I remember
laughing, and wondering if I was loosing my mind, but really believing
I was finding it.

I've never seen a ghost but I talk to god all the time.

I wrote a poem beginning with the line "I Cannot Sleep and the Birds are
Barking" about a dream I had involving a tiny coffin that contained a humming
bird with long tail feathers. I wrote it for my friend, Kathy, who believed that
things—furniture, clothing, dolls, and other physical objects were haunted.

She made sculptures from such objects and was fearful of, and in
love with, the spirits she handled—which made me fearful of, and in
love with, her. Watching her move across Plaza Ferdinand one day, I
thought she looked like Lou Reed.

sun also rises. blending
and calling in colloquial
tongue, "The goose has died"
as Lou Reed's sister for

a Pensacola minute struts through
the park, a tough fucking
artist in love with her
details, she makes art from air

she must find total liberation
if only at lunch
downtown pelicans over sleepy
beer bottles of different shades

of blue say sweet 'I love yous'
to her sublime presence

I have yet to see a ghost but converse with the dead in dreams.

I wrote my first chapbook during a tropical storm named Alberto,
a 3-day weekend, 4th of July. *July: A Meditation on Ted Berrigan*.
As the downtown fireworks and flag-waving festivities got rained-out,
I spent most of those three days joyfully on the front porch sipping
coffee, burning incense, and keeping a detailed journal of my reading
of *So Going Around Cities*, my personal celebration of Independence
Day, my solo homage to the poet on the anniversary of his death.

Jamey Jones lives in Pensacola, FL and is the author of several chapbooks, including *Twelve Windows* (brown boke, 2009), *In The Key of Clothespin* (Fell Swoop, 2021), and the full-length books *Blue Rain Morning* (Farfalla, McMillan and Parrish, 2011) and *morning coffee from the other side* (West Florida Literary Federation, 2021) His work has been published in various journals such as *Zen Monster, Fell Swoop, Mundane Egg, The Brooklyn Rail*, and *Brooklyn Paramount.* He is the editor of Rachael Pongetti's *Uncovering The Layers: The Pensacola Graffiti Bridge Project* (crazy. silly. okay. 2016), and the faculty editor of *Hurricane Review*, the national literary journal of Pensacola State College, where he teaches English, Literature, and Poetry. From 2014 to 2020 he served as the Northwest Florida Poet Laureate.

www.ingramcontent.com/pod-product-compliance
Lightning Source LLC
Chambersburg PA
CBHW051624120626
46551CB00014B/1924